Leadership Mentoring

Maintaining School Improvement in Turbulent Times

Steven Jay Gross

Published in partnership with the
American Association of School Administrators

Rowman & Littlefield Education
Lanham, Maryland • Toronto • Oxford
2006

Published in partnership with the
American Association of School Administrators

Published in the United States of America
by Rowman & Littlefield Education
A Division of Rowman & Littlefield Publishers, Inc.
A wholly owned subsidiary of The Rowman & Littlefield Publishing Group, Inc.
4501 Forbes Boulevard, Suite 200, Lanham, Maryland 20706
www.rowmaneducation.com

PO Box 317
Oxford
OX2 9RU, UK

Copyright © 2006 by Steven Jay Gross

All rights reserved. No part of this publication may be reproduced, stored in a retrieval system, or transmitted in any form or by any means, electronic, mechanical, photocopying, recording, or otherwise, without the prior permission of the publisher.

British Library Cataloguing in Publication Information Available

Library of Congress Cataloging-in-Publication Data

Gross, Steven J.
 Leadership mentoring: maintaining school improvement in turbulent times / Steven Jay Gross.
  p. cm.
 "Published in partnership with the American Association of School Administrators."
 Includes bibliographical references.
 ISBN-13: 978-1-57886-288-7 (hardcover : alk. paper)
 ISBN-13: 978-1-57886-433-1 (pbk. : alk. paper)
 ISBN-10: 1-57886-288-4 (hardcover : alk. paper)
 ISBN-10: 1-57886-433-X (pbk. : alk. paper)
 1. School management and organization. 2. Educational leadership.
 3. Mentoring in education. 4. School improvement programs. I. American Association of School Administrators. II. Title.
 LB2805.G773 2006
 371.2—dc22   2005037853

∞™ The paper used in this publication meets the minimum requirements of American National Standard for Information Sciences—Permanence of Paper for Printed Library Materials, ANSI/NISO Z39.48-1992.
Manufactured in the United States of America.

To my mother, Esther Barg,
and my sister, Barbara Karlin,
with much love

Contents

Acknowledgments — vii

Introduction: Mentoring and the Challenge of Leading in a Turbulent Era — ix

1. A District Confronts a Dilemma — 1
2. Mentoring Educational Leaders—The Big Picture — 11
3. Mentoring, Ethical Decision Making, and Turbulence Theory: Keys to the Model of Leadership Mentoring — 39
4. The Design Team Faces a New Hurdle: Time to Keep It Real — 63
5. The Design Team Builds a Model of Leadership Mentoring — 101
6. Implementation of the Leadership Mentoring Program — 123

Conclusion: The Design Team's Closing Meeting — 131

References — 137

About the Author — 145

Acknowledgments

I want to thank several people who have mentored me in the process of writing this book. Lois Jones and Judy Borelli taught me, by their fine example, how gifted educators practice the craft of leadership mentoring at a reforming school. Joan Poliner Shapiro, my dear friend and colleague at Temple University, was kind enough to allow me to share some of our coauthored work in this book and has encouraged me to in my own development of turbulence theory, which is a central element. Cindy Tursman first saw merit in the idea of a book on this subject and patiently waited until I was able to turn my attention to the project and complete the job. Paul Cacciato has guided the book through to conclusion. My friends at the Vermont Society for the Study of Education have kept me grounded and energized. I also want to thank my students who have shared their own stories of learning to be leaders in their schools, communities, and profession. Finally, to my friends and colleagues in the United States, Canada, the United Kingdom, Taiwan, and Australia who are helping to build the New DEEL (Democratic-Ethical Educational Leadership), I want you to know how much I appreciate your energy in a fine cause and how much you have inspired me in writing this book.

Introduction: Mentoring and the Challenge of Leading in a Turbulent Era

High on a hilltop overlooking Lake Champlain, nestled among the bushes at the corner of the University of Vermont's Ira Allen Chapel, is the final resting place of John Dewey. As many know, Dewey was born in Burlington, Vermont, and was a UVM alumnus. Over the years, when pondering the larger issues in education or just wondering how to be more effective, I have gone to this out-of-the-way place. I even brought classes of students there when I taught at Trinity College of Vermont, only a few blocks away. "Look," I'd explain, "he was quite real. Please understand that." Today I teach at Temple University in Philadelphia but return home to Vermont each week. Now, just as when I worked nearby, I make a regular visit to this place of honor.

The words on Dewey's headstone are particularly relevant for a book on mentoring:

> The things in civilization we most prize are not of ourselves. They exist by grace of the doings and sufferings of the continuous human community in which we are a link. Ours is the responsibility of conserving, transmitting, rectifying and expanding the heritage of values we have received that those who come after us may receive it more solid and secure, more widely accessible and more generously shared than we have received it.
> From: A Common Faith. John Dewey UVM Class of 1879

For me, this quote crystallizes the spirit of mentoring for leadership in the clearest possible way. We are not simply speaking of the career of one individual. Dewey's perspective, which captures his enduring vision for life in and beyond the schoolhouse doors, depicts a flowing civilization and our obligation to take responsibility for our lives, for our link in the chain. It is up to us, as leaders and educators of leaders, to conserve, transmit, rectify, and expand upon conditions that we find as we take on our work. This exhortation is not empty rhetoric, it has a direction: we are charged with leaving conditions better than we found them, so that the next generation may find the best qualities of civilization "more solid and secure, more widely accessible and more generously shared."

Mentoring new leaders is a crucial human task, with purpose and clear goals. It is the hope of this book to show how this message from Dewey can be translated into clear, specific action for those who care about school leaders and the fate of the millions of children in their charge.

WHY LEADERSHIP MENTORING IS NEEDED

My experience with mentoring new professionals started when I began my work as curriculum and staff development director at the Rutland Northeast Supervisory Union in Vermont in 1986. As soon as I arrived, I was asked to help create a mentoring program for new high school teachers. The problem we faced during that time was similar to the problem that readers of this book will find at the principal level: too many new educators were leaving the school too soon, and we worried that we had not done enough to help them find a home in our system. Our response was to develop one of the early examples of teacher mentoring. Each new teacher was provided with a mentor and worked with the school principal and with me to discuss shared readings and think through problems over the course of their first year. This program was designed by a committee including district leaders, board members, the high school's principal, and high school faculty members. The results of the teacher-mentoring program were striking. Instead of losing eight teachers in one year, we were able to keep all of the new teachers that we hired. We dealt with a difficult problem and helped to turn around a demoralizing situation. The Otter Valley Union High School went on to become highly respected for its high-quality, sustained reforms. I believe that the commitment to mentor new teachers was part of that success. I have used a similar kind of committee concept for the development of the leadership mentoring program that I have designed for this book because I know that it can work.

During the same time, I was responsible for supervising teachers in three of our small schools and for advising and coaching the teaching principals of these schools. I learned very quickly that the principal's work is highly complex, often requiring the ability to shift from lofty planning to breaking up a fight in the hallway. Besides these challenges, each of the schools had its own board and budget. Working with all of the other district's principals then, and supervising prospective administrators in their field placements at Temple University now, only helps to underscore the difficulties and the rewards of being a principal. While I know that our program of principal preparation is of high quality, I realize that there is no preservice preparation that can provide even a gifted educator with the experience that she or he will need to succeed. It is clear to me that new principals need and deserve sustained, dependable guidance.

As a researcher I spend time with scores of gifted building leaders and learn many wonderful lessons in the craft and art of being a principal. These educators were great teachers to me and to their faculty, staff, students, parents, and communities. That is why it was so difficult to see them leave eventually, why it was so important to find a superb new principal, and why it was crucial for the new principal to get the kind of support he or she needed to grow into this pivotal position. In *Promises Kept: Sustaining School and District Leadership in a Turbulent Era* (2004) I developed ideas about mentoring school leaders as part of dealing with the problem of leadership succession. I found, however, that the topic was of interest to many practitioners and deserved a good deal more reflection and writing.

Those wishing to become educational leaders at the building level face daunting challenges, some of which are traditional in our field.

How does a teacher become a successful administrator? Do we have a natural progression from the classroom to the principal's desk? Very often we don't. While my own research and that of many others demonstrates the power and promise of shared governance, these examples remain enlightened exceptions. For too many people, the step from the classroom to the principal's office is disjointed, awkward, and altogether intimidating. Getting off on the wrong foot, abandoning the journey, or precluding the chance to lead by earning certification but never pursuing a principal's position is a sad result. We must do better if we are to raise the next generation of school leaders. Recent scholarship in mentoring (Crow and Matthews 1998, Zachary 2000, Daresh 2001, Capasso and Daresh 2001, and Mertz 2004) has done much to begin filling this void with efforts in program design and role clarification.

Yet, I am convinced that our circumstances have changed fundamentally in the past few years, demanding that we create a new kind of leadership mentoring program. We are no longer in the school-restructuring period of the 1990s, when educational experimentation was open and the world seemed equally receptive to rapid, positive transformation. With the continuing press of anti-public-school sentiment coming from the political extremes, the powerful intervention of federal law in the form of No Child Left Behind, and a post–September 11 world, the ground under our feet quakes. This reminds me of the title of Doris Kearns Goodwin's account of the American home front in World War II, *No Ordinary Time*. For schools to be equal to this challenge, we need democratic, ethical leaders. The alternative is to accept the principal as a mere functionary, an obedient manager.

Therefore, this book does not stand for a generic form of leadership. Since we are truly in a turbulent era, filled with ethical dilemmas, a leader who values democratic schooling, based on clear ethical decision making, will, in my opinion, best be able to navigate effectively and support the development of students and faculty. This is not in place of understanding the technical qualities of the job. Those are clearly necessary and are an essential part of this book. However, understanding turbulence and ethical decision making are above and beyond the traditional basics. I believe that they are part of a new requirement for today's principals.

A NOTE ON THE STRUCTURE OF THIS BOOK

Mentoring is complex, and starting a program as important as this is hardly simple. In my experience, content and process are never so crucial as when school systems wish to move into the field of serious change. Because of this belief, I decided to situate the ideas of starting a leadership mentoring program in an imaginary school system. When I say imaginary, please do not assume that I mean factitious in the normal sense of that word. Our superintendent, Betty Clark, her board chair, Antonio Bruski, the Randolph School board, and the group they organize to build a serious leadership mentoring program are fashioned from my own experiences and those I have studied firsthand over the years. The story line is meant to show how people can work together, usually without conflict, to accomplish a difficult task. It is designed to create a more natural, less didactic way of imagining the product and the process of creating a leadership mentoring program because the steps of program development are exposed much as they might be in a real-world situation. As you will see, though their work is of good quality, it is imperfect, and, in the final chapter, they discover a blind spot in the district's overall planning. Although Randolph's case is built upon the need to deal with a high turnover rate among new principals, I would advocate a leadership mentoring program for any new principal, even in districts that have no trouble retaining new principals. The reason is simple: an effective mentoring program for new building leaders is likely to improve their performance at whatever stage of development they may happen to be.

This book aims at answering six fundamental questions:

1. How might a district interested in leadership mentoring organize its work?

2. What background is there in the current literature on leadership mentoring, and how might the literature serve as an effective basis for program development?
3. What theoretical framework can planners use to organize their program so that it will have unity and best respond to the hardest questions facing building leaders?
4. What example of leadership mentoring that uses this theoretical framework can be studied so that we can understand the emerging model in a naturalistic setting?
5. What are the qualities of a fully developed model for leadership mentoring?
6. How might such a program be implemented and connected to larger district priorities?

Each chapter of this book is dedicated to responding to these driving questions.

Chapter 1 lays out the current building-leadership crisis that the Randolph School District is facing. The board chair and superintendent recognize that the attrition rate among new principals is alarming and call for a board retreat on the matter. They leave their retreat with a serious approach to handle it. This chapter is aimed at orienting the reader to the larger context of leadership mentoring, which is the whole question of leadership succession and induction. In addition, the chapter should be helpful to those who feel the need to develop such a program but who are not sure how to organize their program development at the district level.

Chapter 2 takes the program planners (called the Design Team) into their first task, becoming grounded in the literature of leadership mentoring. This includes their report on such topics as demographic changes leading to possible principal shortages, new challenges in the job, and a variety of mentoring programs currently in use in North America and around the world, as well as common qualities of successful programs.

In chapter 3 the Design Team takes a novel step by engaging in a thought experiment. Their purpose is to find a set of central ideas or a theoretical framework on which to organize the leadership mentoring program. Their invented case, showing an ethical dilemma and how a first-year principal and his mentor resolve it, helps to show the concepts of multiple ethical paradigm and turbulence theory as they are used in practice.

Chapter 4 takes the Design Team and the Randolph district to the next stage, to seeing how their theoretical ideas play out in a real case study. This case study, conducted over a period of two years, shows the kind of support and problem solving that a mentor can give to a protégé. It also shows a unique five-step dialogue used by the pair to uncover issues, craft responses, and deal with personal feelings surrounding leadership conflicts. The second part of the case study shows how the concepts of multiple ethical paradigm and turbulence theory operate to resolve ethical dilemmas.

Chapter 5 is where the Design Team must use all of its previous work to build a program, grounded in research, theory, and actual practice. The result is a robust program that requires a great deal of commitment on everyone's part but also holds the potential to resolve the alarming and wasteful problem of losing good new principals.

In chapter 6 the Design Team concludes its work by creating an implementation plan. Here it provides the Randolph board with advice on starting the leadership mentoring program while pointing out the district's immediate need to connect this program to the larger issue of school reform.

The quote on John Dewey's headstone can be read as a test of our ideas in the best sense of that word. Dewey admonished us to "conserve, transmit, rectify and expand the heritage of values" we received so that we pass on something far better to the next generation. In the case of new school principals, I believe that the kind of mentoring detailed in this book, built through community engagement and focused on nurturing ethical decision making, passes Dewey's test because it answers the needs of our field in this era of turbulence and opportunity.

CHAPTER 1

A District Confronts a Dilemma

Randolph was never an easy community in which to run a school system, but things were never like this. As superintendent Betty Clark and school board chair Antonio Bruski met for their biweekly strategy luncheon, they mused over earlier times.

"When you first hired me, I had my hands full, coming from a smaller district. Do you remember?" asked Betty.

Antonio smiled slyly. "I will never forget that look on your face at the first full board meeting! You'd never been on television before and that crowd of angry parents was a surprise for all of us. What was their issue? Something like the basketball coach not putting in everyone in a game, even when we were way ahead. You looked straight at me as if to say, 'Give me a break! I did not come here, leave my good job, and move my family three hundred miles for this!' I felt very sorry to introduce you to our community that way."

"It took some time to settle in," replied Betty. "But then we started to calm things down, and I got a sense of this place and all of you. There was also a strong administrative team in place to help all of us turn our plans into real change for our children. But that was seven years ago. We both know what's happened since then."

"Do we ever!" Antonio's eyes widened.

"Look, I know it's hard to hire great principals and keep them, but we've been through nine principals in our ten schools in the past few years. That is simply too much. We've got teachers who no longer trust that their new leader will be there very long. Parents are feeling the same way. And you know what? I don't blame them a bit. How can the board and I move the district toward our goals if this keeps up? Right now, we're getting the reputation of a place that chews up its building administrators and spits them out. That only makes it harder to recruit. What's going on?"

"I'm not sure, Betty. Maybe it's bad luck or poor hiring decisions, but I don't trust those answers. No, we've got a problem here, and it's worrying the board just as much as it's worrying you."

"Right! We need to turn this around quickly, but we need more than a Band-Aid approach. I'd like to do some thinking and planning at the board retreat next month, and I hope to come out of that with a plan of action. This is just too important for us to let go."

Antonio responded with a smile and a simple, "Agreed."

The issue was out in the open and its importance was obvious. Randolph's board had worked effectively together with Dr. Clark for years. They had dealt with hot issues during that time including high-stakes testing, multicultural education, and the ever present budget crunch. They also knew that their most important job as board members was not to decide where to purchase new tires for the bus fleet or what a fair price for heating oil was. Their job was to establish policy, and perhaps their most significant job was to bring excellent leaders to their school system to carry out district policy priorities. That is why the rapid turnover of Randolph's principals was so startling to the board and administration. Without stability and wisdom at the building level, all of their work was in jeopardy. As Ruth Dyer, the most senior member of the board, put it, "You can ask a lot out of teachers, kids, and the community. You can ask them to work harder, contribute extra hours for a good cause. You can even ask them to prepare for some of these silly tests we use too many of, if they understand that we have not lost sight of what real learning is all about. But," she said as she eyed everyone at the table, "you'd better not let them think you've forgotten how to find them a good leader! That they won't stand for. They're annoyed with us now and they have every right. I'm not blaming Betty. Just the opposite. I'm with you and Antonio and the rest of you when you say that this issue is our top priority."

With the issue of retaining top-quality principals on the table, plans for the board retreat started to fall into place. A date was set and a facilitator from a local university was contacted. His job was to shed light on the high rate of principal turnover and provide his best guess as to why Randolph was having such a problem. Betty and Antonio reasoned that a thoughtful analysis was required as a first step before any action was contemplated. A good deal rested on the success of the retreat. Betty Clark was counting on more than some simple response to the issue. She and her board were looking for a strategy to change their approach to hiring and nurturing new school leaders.

THE RANDOLPH SCHOOL BOARD RETREAT

Everyone at the board retreat seemed a bit on edge as Professor Grey began his presentation. Sam Grey was a trusted figure in Randolph by this time since he had come up through the administrative ranks himself in a neighboring district and since he was a down-to-earth scholar who had helped these leaders in earlier dilemmas. Grey's home now was at Acropolis University, a large research institution situated in an urban setting. This was helpful to the board as well since it meant that they could tap into many resources and a broad perspective on their current problem.

Sam cleared his throat, a little self-consciously, to get the crowd's attention. While they focused, he mused that working with an anxious board was altogether different from moving a new class of doctoral students to the next level of understanding organizational theory. These were people in need of tangible facts, and time was always short.

"Good evening, everyone. Look, I have seen your agenda for tonight and I realize that my presentation is only part of the first dozen items that you need to consider during this retreat. We've all had a long workday already so, if you don't mind, I'll get right to my findings." Two or three board members smiled to each other. It was this kind of direct talk that they appreciated. Grey might work at the university, but he was anything but woolly-headed.

"You've asked me to try to make sense out of a hard situation you are facing, namely what might the departing principals have in common? The point we are all looking for is obvious—if we can find such a pattern, we may be a step closer to finding a reasonable response. Anyway," Sam smiled a little sheepishly, "that was the theory.

"I have taken a careful look at every principal whose tenure at Randolph was less than three years, and, as you know, there have been quite a few of these individuals recently. I have considered their qualifications, their longevity in previous jobs, and the circumstances in each of the schools they led while they were here, and I've interviewed those who met with these principals for exit interviews. Where possible, I interviewed the departed principals themselves. Finally, I've done a literature review so that I can compare your district to others around the country and compare the scope of your problem to that faced by others. Based on all of that background checking, I can tell you a few things.

"First, you do have a serious problem in this area. It is getting worse and it is occurring at a very bad time demographically. What I mean is, your ability to keep principals is far weaker than that of comparable districts in other parts of the state, region, and nation. You were right to worry. Not only that, but the problem seems to be building over time. The pattern in Randolph is for ever faster principal turnover. Placed in the larger context, your district appears to be less attractive to new principals just at a time when districts are competing to fill these positions. This obviously places you at a serious disadvantage. The very people you want to attract, bright women and men, will have the most options, and Randolph will not look very good to them. They will be the first to ask probing questions and find out that this pattern of principal turnover is a strike against you."

"All right Sam, we understand that things are serious. Is there any good news about the situation, something that can point to a direction out of this mess?" Antonio was speaking for everyone in the room.

"Right, you know me and you know that I like to get the bad news out first. Well there clearly are some good aspects to this problem that you need to understand. First, none of the hires seems to have been a mistake, at least not from the point of view of background and preparation. These were top-flight candidates with solid records in previous jobs, and a pattern of impressive professional education. I can't lay the blame for this problem on the board or on the superintendent. You did the hiring part of the job well. Equally, you did not send these new principals into nightmare schools. While none of the people in question had more than five years' prior experience as a principal, you sent the most seasoned to the more challenging schools and sent the less experienced administrators to schools that were very stable. Those were wise decisions, in my opinion. That should make you feel better but you are probably wondering, if the right people were hired and were sent to situations that were a reasonable match, what went wrong? That is what was bothering me too.

"That brings me to perhaps my best piece of news: there *is* something that you can do about the problem. You see, what these people had in common, besides a good résumé, was the feeling of isolation and a lack of support once they were in place. Now, before you jump to conclusions, I am not speaking about Dr. Clark's work. Everyone volunteered that she was a good supervisor of her principals. They felt that she understood their situations, helped to find resources, and was supportive. Far from being the problem, she encouraged the best of these principals to stay a while longer. In my opinion, they needed something more than a good superintendent to report to. They needed, but did not receive, sustained mentoring, and that is a different issue."

"What are you talking about? What do we have to do, hold their hands and baby people? We are hiring leaders, and leaders should take care of themselves!" Andy Sparkinburg was not used to this kind of meeting and this was not the way that he ran his business in town.

"No, Andy, we are not talking about hand-holding or making excuses for leaders. What I mean by mentoring is a practice of putting a system of guidance into place that just might help principals to stay on the job long enough to become established. Randolph may not have a mentoring program in place for its principals, but you do have an induction program for every new teacher; that is a state guideline and a requirement of your accreditation board. I am talking about setting something up like that for principals as well. You won't be the first or only ones to think about this; it's a growing trend.

"But," Sam became more serious than before, "I must warn you. The idea of real mentoring is not a light thing. You've seen this when other districts have gone through the motions with teachers' mentoring novice colleagues. They may call these mentoring programs but they are only superficial and mechanical. Nothing is really invested and, as a consequence, nothing serious is ever gained."

Seeing where this was going, Betty Clark stepped in. "What you're saying, Sam, is that we have a pronounced challenge on our hands that merits our best, not some knee-jerk response." Not waiting for a loss of momentum, Betty continued. "If we are going to give this our best shot, I would advise the board to take this as seriously as you do, say, a building project. We need a high-powered but small task force with a specific charge, decent resources, and a limited amount of time. It's now mid-July. My question to you is this: can we have agreement for a top-flight principal mentoring program by January 1 of next year? That way, we can have it built into next year's budget and be able to use this as an enticement to any new hires we make next spring."

Antonio was thinking this through as he spoke. "This sounds pretty reasonable to me. Do I hear a motion?"

The board debated the specifics for only a short while and then put the matter to a vote. The end result met all of Betty's conditions. Instead of a task force, Randolph would have a design team. Martin Ulner thought that the term "task force" was entirely too militaristic as well as trite. The board further specified that the superintendent and the board chair would be responsible to meet regularly with the design team, bring their work to the full board on a regular basis, and communicate board reactions and suggestions to the design team. Finally, the board took Betty's phrase "high-powered" to heart when they agreed on the design team's composition. Betty was asked to make sure that the group included an elementary school principal, a high school principal, a university faculty member, the assistant superintendent for personnel and staff development, a parent, and a board member.

At their next luncheon meeting, Betty and Antonio worked through the possibilities and came up with a list of candidates. The administrators were the easiest to identify and to get on board since they were directly touched by the issue. Finding the right parent and board member was a bit trickier. As for the university faculty member, it turned out that Sam Grey's research on what he called leadership mentoring was so closely aligned with their issue that he was happy to participate.

The time had come for Antonio and Betty to meet with the design team, charge them with their task, and get this project started. Within three weeks of the board's retreat, the date was set and the design team had its first meeting. Betty and Antonio sat together at the head of the table. "It's good to have you all here and we all appreciate the help you've agreed to give to our district." Betty spoke in her ceremonial voice. This whole project was a bit of a gamble, she knew, and she wanted everyone in the room to be prepared for a difficult assignment. "We know that you care about mentoring or we would never have asked you to join us. The board needs a workable, affordable plan by January 1 so that it can be up and running at the start of next school year. That gives your group four months. Not much time, but we think it's enough."

"Betty and I aren't just here to charge the group with its mission," Antonio added, "We will be here each month to see how you're doing, to read over your work carefully, and to be your contact with the board and the community. We are as committed as you are."

The charge was spelled out next. By the start of the next calendar year, the design team needed to produce a leadership mentoring plan for new principals that contained five elements:

1. Clear context for leadership mentoring showing background and any relevant research
2. Guiding principles or theories for Randolph's program
3. An example or carefully selected case study of this kind of program already tried out in practice, if at all possible
4. A clear model of the program itself flowing logically from mentoring's context, guiding principles, and case study
5. Specific advice on program implementation

Betty saw that the mood in the room had turned more serious than she expected. "Look, I know that this is a large amount of work. I also know that it might sound easier for us simply to copy someone else's program and paste it onto our district."

"Well, to tell you the truth, Betty," Ronnie Foldrona, the high school principal, wanted to make her point right away, "this is a bit more intense that I had planned on. I mean, you are talking about a real research project. I know that Sam does this sort of thing for a living and he may have the time for it as well. You know what my life is like. I mean, wouldn't it really be better for us to simply steal the best thing out there and plug it in here?"

"Ronnie, you're right to worry about time, and, believe me, I have no intention of asking our building leaders to waste one minute; there is simply too much to do. We went around and around on this at the board and in private before even coming to the design team. Even if we wanted to adopt some ready-made plan, how would we decide which to select? What is working? What fits us best? In the end it seemed that the biggest risk as far as wasting time would be to rush into someone else's plan only to find out that it was not right for our situation. We are in trouble on this issue because we did not plan carefully for the support of new principals. I hope that the design team will take these months and make sure that we don't fall into that trap again." Betty was sure that she had made her best case, even though she sympathized with Ronnie's time dilemma.

"When you put it that way, I guess that makes sense. I will need to work with you on some of my other 'projects' and find ways to balance my schedule. I can't simply add one more thing." Ronnie's point was made, and Betty understood it at once. Too often the best administrators were asked to work ever harder on new projects without being released from old obligations.

"Agreed," Sam spoke up. "There are elements of the charge that fit pretty well with some of my research, as I told you when you called me the other week. Ronnie's right as well, this is the kind of work that I do pretty regularly. It might work best if we think about the task and how responsibilities may be divided. It is a big challenge, I understand, but it may be easier if we take it piece by piece and see where it leads us."

Sam probably knew that anyone who has a constructive idea in a meeting such as this is very likely to be asked to take on a new responsibility, and that is exactly the way things turned out. In the end, the design team nominated and elected two cochairs, Ronnie and Sam. The match made sense since both had worked together on smaller projects and since together they represented a balance between district and community. Equally important, each had impressive knowledge and resources to bring to the task. Finally, the design team shared e-mail addresses and decided to ask the district's director of technology to create a Web page so that they could start to share ideas with the wider community immediately.

Betty and Antonio walked out of the meeting together. "What do you think?" asked a tired superintendent.

"It was a little tense at first. I mean, Ronnie is not cynical or burned out but we almost slipped into a pattern that neither you nor I like very much."

"Well, it is easy for us to simply keep on asking for more and to forget about what a principal's life is like. That is exactly what this mentoring program is designed to correct. Ronnie is a seasoned pro; we both are more than happy to have her. I wonder whether or not this program may have something in it for her as well. At any rate, we are on the way to something that feels responsive to our problem. That's crucial."

"And," the board chair added, "we are both in this for the duration. I think that everyone involved has signed on to something pretty powerful."

CHAPTER 2

Mentoring Educational Leaders—The Big Picture

THE DESIGN TEAM COMES INTO ITS OWN

With only four months to go from having no plan to a working mentoring program, the Design Team understood that there was no time to waste. With Betty Clark's help the team was given office space when needed, someone to keep notes, and access to high-speed Internet computers. They decided to put off the Web page until there were preliminary reports to share. The exchange of e-mails, however, was immediate. In addition, the Design Team agreed to adopt their name formally—to capitalize it and to add their names to all e-mail correspondence so that the wider community would know who was involved in this work.

Sam Grey did follow through on his offer to help lead the first part of the charge. With the help of a graduate student, Sam built a database of articles and reports on mentoring in the United States and abroad. Then he and Ronnie met to work out a reasonable way to structure the rest of the task. With four other members of the Design Team able to contribute, they divided the readings by theme and asked each person to return one week later with a summary of the highlights of the assigned section. In round-robin sessions, each person shared his or her findings with the rest of the group. Some time was given at the end of each report to question or challenge one another. With the help of the note taker, a common set of transcripts was available, but Sam guessed correctly that he would be the one to pull the pieces together.

"Look, everyone," Sam smiled, knowing that his offer would be taken up at once. "If it's just the same to you, I'll do my best at writing a rough draft. What I will need from each of you is a close reading of your own section as well as help with the introduction and especially the conclusion. Okay?" No one in the room even considered objecting.

The result, after everyone became familiar with e-mail attachments, was surprisingly successful. The group established useful protocols such as placing their initials at the top of drafts they had edited and writing their own changes in boldface (using the software's built-in ability to flag changes in drafts would come later). More significantly, they visited websites that Sam Grey's research had unearthed and began a habit that would last throughout the project of sharing new findings with the rest of the group.

When it came time to share their first assignment with Betty and Antonio, two things were clear. The Design Team members took ownership of their work and were proud of their process. While anxious to hear of ways to improve the report, they were surprised and pleased with the quality they were able to achieve in just a matter of a few weeks.

Ronnie started the meeting with Betty and Antonio. "Welcome to both of you and hello again to our regulars!" Betty and Antonio both thought this did not sound like the same hesitant high school principal they had met with when the Design Team started its work. The extra help that Betty gave Ronnie and the extended deadline on a few of her reports for the central office might have been very useful indeed.

Ronnie continued, "From the e-mails that we've copied to you over the past few weeks, you may have a good sense of the process we've created so far. Thanks to everyone, especially Sam, for helping us to get results. I want to share one other part of our strategy that Betty and Antonio might not know since it came out of a conference call that we had last night to prepare for this afternoon's meeting with you both. I am about to pass out our draft reply to the first part of our charge. Before Sam explains how we've organized this, I want you to know that we have called it our first report. We have decided to fashion our work in this way: Each month, roughly, we will share a draft report that responds to a charge from our mission. Each will be designed to be a freestanding unit as well as a mutually supporting part of the whole. In this way, even if something unforeseen happens and we don't end up establishing a leadership mentoring program next year, our work will not have been wasted. The reports can still be used in other district activities."

"Okay," Betty thought to herself, "this sounds like a group that values its time and likes its work. Not bad for a start."

Sam took his turn next. "When we first thought about the problem of context for the mentoring program, we discussed the need for background. The point of this report is to make sure that we build our program with full awareness of the options and never by default. This draft is our best shot at answering these questions:

- What difficulties do today's principals face that make mentoring a relevant idea?
- Where does the idea of mentoring come from?
- What models exist for leadership mentoring programs in the United States and abroad?
- What qualities should mentoring programs embody?

With that overview, let me pass around our report."

THE DESIGN TEAM'S RESPONSE TO CHARGE 1 FROM THE BOARD

We are working on a complex problem facing educational leaders today, namely, how to support and retain high-quality principals in a time of high job-related stress in many schools in the United States. This report seeks to establish a foundation for future program planning by looking into these issues:

1. What difficulties do today's principals face that make mentoring a relevant idea?

2. Where does the idea of mentoring come from?
3. What models exist for leadership mentoring programs in the United States and abroad?
4. What qualities should mentoring programs embody?

1. WHAT DIFFICULTIES DO TODAY'S PRINCIPALS FACE THAT MAKE MENTORING A RELEVANT IDEA?

Our review of research teaches us that, while being a principal has never been easy, there are reasons to believe that additional help will be needed to secure the next generation of principals.

Shortage of Replacements for Principals

One of the first things that becomes clear to those studying the issue of the principalship is that we are in the midst of a generational turnover in building leadership. Looking at educational administrators as a group, the U.S. Department of Labor's Bureau of Labor Statistics states that in 2002 there were 427,000 jobs held in the field. While this included all educational administrators in public and private practice and at all levels, a large proportion worked in the public K–12 school system (United States Department of Labor 2005). Currently, it is estimated that there are 93,200 school principals in the United States (Blackman & Fenwick 2000, cited in Crocker & Harris 2002). This large group of school leaders is in the midst of a changing of the guard. Since 1993, we have known that 55% of school principals planned to retire within a decade (NAESP/NASSP 1998). Simply looking at the average age of sitting principals tells a good deal of the story. In 1993 the average age of principals was 47.7. Thiry-seven percent of principals were already over age 50 (NAESP/NASSP 1998). The aging of our building leaders is a clear national pattern.

In New York City, for example, approximately 1,100 schools face the retirement of 260 principals, and half of the schools are run by people with less than three years' experience as principals (as of 2002) (Archer 2002).

No level of the K–12 system is free from the threat of principal shortage, according to the studies. Only 9% of elementary schools across the United States stated that there was a surplus of qualified principal candidates, for instance, while 47% stated that there was a shortage. In the case of middle schools and high schools, the situation is worse. In both of these, only 6% responded that they had a surplus of candidates and 55% found themselves facing a shortage (NAESP/NASSP/ERS 1998).

Thomas F. Koerner, executive director of the National Association of Secondary School Principals in 1998, stated, "Schools are going without principals, retired principals are being called back to full time work and districts have to go to great lengths to recruit qualified candidates" (Hopkins 1998).

While principal-preparation programs produce certified graduates, many of these people choose not to seek administrative positions (NAESP/NASSP/ERS 1998). This leads us to the question, why are people electing not to become principals just when we need a new generation of building leaders?

Pressures Faced by Today's Principals

The job of principal has never been an easy one (Aiken 2002). However, recent research has cast new light on traditional job pressures while revealing new conflicts in the role.

Lashway (2003) describes specific causes of stress in new leaders that bear watching:

- Complexity. The job of principal is complex. Simply put, the principal is asked to work rapidly on issues ranging from bus schedules to safety to performance on academics. The obvious problem of juggling multiple issues that vary in priority requires a blend of wisdom and maturity. New people are unlikely to possess these qualities at the start of their careers in administration.

- Isolation. When a new teacher comes into the profession, she or he enters into a building filled with experienced colleagues. The confusion of the first several years is normal and we do lose too many promising new educators during that period. However, imagine the situation facing new principals where there are no colleagues in the building with similar responsibilities. Even in the district context, there may not be a collegial relationship among the principals. This means that the principal's isolation is hardwired into the job description in most districts.
- Lonely job. Coming from the ranks of teachers, it might be natural to suppose that one will maintain a warm collegial relationship with faculty after becoming a principal. This is often not the case. Becoming an administrator often means an immediate switch from being one of "us" to becoming one of "them." This, logically enough, means a lonely life to too many school principals. The very same personality traits that made a person attractive during the hiring process, such as superb human-relation skills, can make a people person susceptible to feeling lonely. As one writer put it, "Voices stop when you walk into the teachers' lounge" (Diane Curtis in Lashway 2003).
- Assimilation. There are no generic schools since each school has its own context. The community each school serves has a history, traditions, and an evolving set of accomplishments and challenges. Each school system has its own evolution of norms and forces propelling it. For the new principal, the question is, how are things done and how are they done here (Crow & Matthews 1998)? Without clear guidance, how is a new leader to know? With the press of this complex job, when is there time for a person to become familiar with the rich history and mores of the school unaided?

- Role conflict. The job of the principal also has a series of potentially conflicting demands. Are school goals aligned with district goals? If not, how does a building principal support her school without getting into trouble with the district? Does the principal find that the school's reform agenda is reasonable and in keeping with his philosophy? Looking at the national picture, can the principal be effective in dealing with such issues as adequate yearly progress on the one hand and support hands-on instruction or multidisciplinary investigation on the other? Is the principal merely an agent from the district or state, or is she a professional with deeply held beliefs based upon ethical reasoning (Gross & Shapiro 2004)?

Of course, there is much more to the job of principal than these five areas of stress. Still, these issues alone make it clear that, for many, being the person on the other side of the principal's desk is not an easy career move. In short, this is not an attractive job to people who are otherwise qualified. Added to this, other writers point out that there is too much reliance on on-the-job training for new principals (Brown, Anfara, Hartman, Mahar, & Mills 2001).

New Leadership Demographics

Another important trend is the rise in the number of women and heretofore underrepresented minority group members in the principalship. In 1988, only 2% of principals were women. By 2000, 35% of all principals were women (Malone 2001, referring to Blackman & Fenwick 2000). At that time, 13% of principals were members of minority groups. Younger women and minority group members, who were so underrepresented in building and district leadership roles so recently, cannot depend upon mentors who share their backgrounds and who know, from life experiences, their struggles. Yet, the good news that leadership positions are more available to women and minority group members helps to point out a striking need for quality and sensitive mentoring that incorporates diversity as a crucial value.

2. WHERE DOES THE IDEA OF MENTORING COME FROM?

Clearly, districts face a serious problem of securing the services of qualified leaders now and in the near-term future. With a generational turnover increasing the need to find principals on the one hand and a job that comes across as increasingly unattractive on the other hand, it is doubly important to make sure that school systems do everything possible to keep promising new leaders. One strategy that makes sense to the Design Team is mentoring for new principals. Mentoring is an ancient concept whose name dates back to Homer's *Odyssey*. Boon (1998) reminds us that Mentor was entrusted with watching over King Odysseus's son Telemachus while Odysseus was at war. In modern times, businesses have used mentoring as a way of helping junior-level employees advance. In educational administration, the practice of mentoring is well known among aspiring principals. Daresh and Playko (1993) make the connection between educational and business mentoring. They also report satisfaction that mentors experience in their new roles as teachers of a new generation as well as the need to study how these relationships are formed and maintained.

Uneven Support

For principals and assistant principals, Dunavin's 2004 study of a "large, essentially urban and culturally diverse public school district" in the southwest United States (student enrollment of 85,000) found that of the 118 principals and assistant principals returning surveys, 27% participated in formal induction programs for new administrators. Sixty percent received mentoring as part of their induction. Seventy-five percent of principals received mentoring as part of their induction in year one. Thirty-three percent of new assistant principals had the same kind of support.

3. WHAT MODELS EXIST FOR LEADERSHIP MENTORING PROGRAMS IN THE UNITED STATES AND ABROAD?

While mentoring may be an idea with a long history in and outside of educational settings, we believe that it is important to learn from concrete examples. The purpose of the following section is not to attempt an exhaustive review of existing mentoring programs but to provide some examples that may be helpful to planners who want to learn about options. Below, we will examine specific mentoring programs to consider part of the range of possible approaches to this process.

A District-Based Program:
Beginning Principals' Mentoring Program

This program comes from Prince George's County, Maryland (Bundy & McKay 2004), which is the 19th-largest school district in the United States, including 193 schools and 135,000 students.

The Beginning Principals' Mentoring Program was organized in 1998 with the cooperation of the University of Maryland in response to a state and county superintendent request for help. The program included 113 new principals in five cohorts. The size of cohort ranged from 15 to 27 as of 2004 and lasted 18 months. There are five content areas for mentors and protégés including:

1. Instructional leadership (knowledge of research on teaching methodology, curriculum, instructional strategies, and assessment)
2. Supervision and evaluation of teachers
3. Data analysis

4. Shared decision making (with teachers and parents, planning by the whole group)
5. School reform and continuous improvement

A Regional Mentoring Plan: The Journaling Triad

Some mentoring programs grow out of individual contacts and needs. In New York State such a support network developed between three administrators. While they were superintendents, their collegial support could work just as easily for building principals in the same district or between districts. In this case, the journaling triad, as they called themselves, agreed to write four times each week. In this way, a flow of communication was developed as well as an increasing level of understanding. As the e-mail dialogue deepened, it became clear that this small network of support was helpful in the daily tasks of leadership. As one member said, "It's a safe environment to get some really critical feedback."

International Examples of Mentoring

Since the challenge of helping new principals succeed is shared by schools everywhere, it is not surprising that some of the most interesting examples of mentoring programs come from the international community.

Southworth (1995) studied the use of mentors to help new school leaders in Britain. He found that mentoring helped new leaders overcome isolation and allowed the pair (mentor and protégé) to "consider and reconsider" events. Problems regarding mentoring included finding a compatible pair and making sure that mentoring leads to better preparation for schools in the future rather than socializing a new generation to the practices of the past. Boon (1998) studied 27 pairs of mentors and protégés in Singapore and found that mentors felt they improved their professional knowledge by taking on their new roles and that protégés became part of a wider network of colleagues while developing greater self-confidence. Coleman and colleagues (1996) also studied mentoring practices for new and aspiring school leaders in the United Kingdom and Singapore and reported that in the British schools, new leaders appreciated working with a nonjudgmental colleague. He also found important differences between the two systems, such as duration of the mentoring process. Erasmus and Westhuizen (1994) wrote guidelines for mentoring new principals in South Africa and advised that mentors' tasks should include consulting, guiding, and role modeling.

An Example of a Mentoring Program from New Zealand: First Time Principals Programme

The First Time Principals Programme (www.aukland.ac.nz/firstprincipals) includes two hundred new principals who work with 22 highly experienced mentors. A strong emphasis is placed on interpersonal skills, and the program is part of a national educational network. The University of Auckland conducts training for the principals, often in the form of residential courses.

For three half days per year the protégés and mentors work together, using e-mail and telephone conversations between meetings. By design, the First Time Principals Programme concentrates on issues selected by the new principals. "If a mentoring relationship is working well, then the mentor can see if the principal is under stress, talk with them about it and advise them where to seek additional help" (David Eddy, project director of the First Time Principals Programme, in Nelson 2003).

4. WHAT QUALITIES SHOULD MENTORING PROGRAMS EMBODY?

Clearly there are many choices in mentoring-program structure open to our district. We felt that this was important to make everyone aware of since we do not want to create a program by default, that is, by not knowing what some of the possibilities are. However, there is a related question that needs to be answered by any group responsible for designing a responsive mentoring program: What common qualities do successful models possess? We believe that it is crucial for the board and the public to understand our concern for this approach since it may sound a little theoretical. One way for us to consider our task would be to find a program in a district similar to our own and simply copy it. This would certainly increase the speed of our response and there was some discussion of that strategy. After a little reflection, however, we rejected this idea, primarily because we believed that the board had asked us for a thoroughly considered plan with a strong rationale. We decided that we could not impose someone else's mentoring plan any more than we could impose someone else's building design. It was not a blueprint we wanted so much as the equivalent of the building codes that would yield a secure program structure. What we elected to do was to distill the elements of the best advice for any plan. While we don't want to simply use a cookie-cutter approach, we need to share the principles. In this way, we are not stamping out a copy, we are projecting the essential elements of design.

The literature shows us that to be successful, we need to keep five program qualities in mind.

1. First, we need to remember the big picture as we plan. Where does mentoring fit into the larger work of bringing new leaders into our district? Where might we need to watch out for potential downsides to mentoring?
2. Next, we need to understand that good mentors share specific qualities. Many assert that not everyone is destined to be a teacher. The same is true for mentoring. It is imperative for us to know the dispositions of effective mentors regardless of program structure.
3. Third, once we identify potential mentors, we must know how to prepare them for their work. What are effective professional development strategies for this group?

4. Fourth, matching mentors with protégés is not a simple task, and the literature helps us to understand this process better.
5. Finally, we need some practical advice on such specifics as program length and cost.

Seeing the Big Picture

While the task at hand is the creation of a successful leadership mentoring program, we need to step back and recognize this as one piece in the larger picture of leadership development, recruitment, and induction. Our mentoring program will mean little without these efforts, since we must have a clear understanding of larger issues like leadership succession (see Gross 2004), for example. Replacing a leader who has done an effective job is a difficult task; finding the best person to succeed a less-than-remarkable leader is even more challenging. We advise the board to consider the state of each school as it approaches the job of identifying the traits needed for school leaders, and we argue that this is their most important job as representatives of the community. Finding new leaders is a serious expense in time, money, and organizational energy.

Once a recruitment process is under way, we need to have an attitude that will promote mutual benefit. The best candidates will likely have many choices, and, at our best, we expect to be in the same situation. Candidates rightly assume that they will have to compete for a position in one of our schools; we need to understand that we too compete for these people. In this way, our recruitment needs to focus on a fit between a candidate's skills and the needs of our school at the time of the search. There will not be a generic or universally appropriate candidate for our schools just as there is no universally perfect school for the aspiring administrator.

After the conclusion of the hiring process, which includes successfully working through salary and benefit negotiations, we start what is considered the induction process. This term (Lashway 2003) refers to the integration of the new school leader into our district.

The Design Team cautions the board on the overuse of this term, however. As Morgan (1997) informs us, each metaphor illuminates and obscures. Induction as a metaphor illuminates the process by making us aware that we need to bring an outsider into our system as an intentional act, that is, to recognize that the transition into our system will not occur by accident or through osmosis. Taking responsibility for organizing the transition of a new principal into our system is at the heart of our rationale for developing a mentoring system in the first place. Ironically, the term "induction" also obscures reality. We could say that our induction process was haphazard at best in the past and part of the reason for our poor record of keeping promising new school leaders.

Yet, induction, taken out of context, brings to mind entering the military or similar organization. In that case, the organization demands change from the individual with little apparent room for reciprocal change expected because a new person has joined the group. This may be appropriate for some organizations but is not what we are looking for in our schools. First, we are not running an authoritarian organization but an institution whose central mission is the promotion of a democratic way of life. Schools do, and must continue to, cultivate life skills for our students, chief among these being the ability to find and keep meaningful employment. However, it is the more difficult challenge of engaging responsibly in a democratic society that remains our primary goal. As such, we must honor relationships that are mutual in character. Certainly, we have much to share with any new person joining our district, from the new student and his or her family to the new school principal. But we would be missing the spirit of democratic life if we ignored the fact that all newcomers have much to offer our organization. Their perspective, their experiences, their needs and aspirations are all part of what should define us in the future, if we really believe in the equality of people. Induction, looked at in this way, is inadequate for the task of mutual development. We need to have a process that welcomes and educates the new person to our system but that also honors the new person by listening and responding to the energy and goals of each new person, and *changing* accordingly. Perhaps we need to augment the concept of induction with the concept of *development*.

Potential Downsides

Here is another irony. While we believe that mentoring is a powerful idea that holds many potential benefits for our school system, we need to be aware of the dangers of the concept of mentoring as well. Crow and Matthews (1998) suggest three downsides. First, mentors can have selfish or ulterior motives (Muse, Wasden, & Thomas 1988). Why someone wishes to become a mentor is a personal and powerful question that we need to consider. Next, mentors can be too protective (Daresh & Playko 1993), which means that program designers need to be aware of the subtle difference between a generative behavior on the part of the mentor and one that smothers the protégé. Third, mentors may have too much attachment to a single style of leadership, thereby limiting the protégé's originality (Hay 1995, Hart 1991). An additional, fourth, area of caution is the possibility of mentors being too controlling (Lashway 2003). As we mentioned above, a fifth area of concern is that mentoring might be merely bent on molding a new person to the needs of our district. In that way, mentoring can become something that replicates the machine metaphor (Morgan 1997). While we are cautious about the behaviors of the mentor, we must accept that not every person will make a suitable protégé. We will discuss the qualities of a good protégé below but need to state here that both parties must make a sincere commitment to the process.

Finally, based on everything we have said, looking at leadership mentoring as a panacea is a danger. Our enthusiasm for mentoring is moderated by our understanding that it is but one element in the professional development process and not a stand-alone cure-all. The fact that "mentoring" has become a kind of catchphrase today means that too many people may be expecting too much. We believe that this is illogical and possibly places this very promising idea among the fads that have haunted other innovations in education.

Qualities of a Good Mentor

We just enumerated personal qualities that make someone a poor mentor. But a skilled mentor is not merely an educator who is not burdened with these drawbacks; the literature shows us important qualities that we need to look for as we bring our program to life. We need to identify people who are trusted guides (Homer), teachers (Levinson, Darrow, Klein, Levinson, & McKee 1978), sponsors (Schein 1978), challengers (Daloz 1983), and confidants (Gehrke & Kay 1984), according to Crow and Mathews (1998). Others have emphasized qualities such as acceptance of multiple alternative solutions to complex problems, decisiveness, and the habit of asking the right question (Wunsch 1994), and mutual trust (Enz 1992, Daresh and Playko 1992).

Finally, it is imperative for us to clearly describe what we mean by mentoring. We should be careful to define mentoring and careful to distinguish it from related but distinct forms of what Mertz (2004) calls "supportive relationships" (543). Drawing on a broad selection of mentoring literature, Mertz develops a conceptual model that significantly clarifies what mentoring means in terms of intent and involvement. According to this model, we must consider two concepts related to mentoring, namely, the intent of the mentor and the degree of involvement. At the base of the triangular model, the intent is one of modeling and the degree of involvement is one of the role model, peer pal, or supporter (involvement level 1) or teacher or coach (involvement level 2). Higher up is the intent of advising, matched with the involvement of the counselor, adviser, or guide (involvement level 3). At the top of the intent hierarchy is the role of the broker and the intent of the sponsor or benefactor (involvement level 4), the patron or protector (involvement level 5) finally placing the involvement of the mentor at the very top. Clearly, Mertz makes mentoring a most serious enterprise filled with the deepest commitments. While the Design Team will consider this perspective in greater detail as we build the model for our own mentoring program, it is important to state at this early phase of our work that the very definition of mentoring matters. On one hand, if any helping relation is considered mentoring, then we may simply be building a superficial plan that will disappoint everyone. On the other hand, if mentoring is defined as too demanding, we may find it difficult to recruit mentors willing to dedicate the emotional effort to live up to such weighty responsibilities. Lincoln (1999) describes four levels of mentoring. We are probably working on the fourth level: *collegial and collaboration*. The Design Team appreciates thoughtful writers like Mertz and Lincoln for raising the issue of definition.

Clearly the selection of mentors is going to be a crucial element of any program. While the Design Team will incorporate specific steps to identify and recruit mentors, we may also want to use techniques already available. For instance, Geismar, Morris, and Lieberman (2000) speak of a Mentor Identification Instrument used to screen for those with the likely qualities of a good mentor. This is also mentioned by Malone in connection with the Haberman Urban Principal Selection Interview (see Haberman & Dill 1999). The goal seems to be to identify great potential principals for urban schools and pair them up with likely good mentors.

It is no surprise that much has been written about the qualities of a good mentor since that person is central to the whole enterprise. Part of the challenge for those wishing to design an effective program is to remember that the qualities of good mentors described above are ones that many people may think they possess since they reflect the values of a caring, committed person. Planners must seek ways to find evidence of these qualities in the *performance* of mentor candidates as they have lived their professional lives. This implies making the role of mentor so prestigious that highly talented and motivated leaders will aspire to it.

Qualities of a Good Protégé

While we naturally spend a good deal of time thinking through what personality traits make for an effective mentor, we should also be concerned with the qualities of a good protégé. Looked at one way, this may seem unnecessary since any new principal will likely be required to participate in the leadership mentoring program. However, we believe that merely going through the motions of the program will be a waste of time. What should be brought into the hiring decision itself is this question: does this person approach his or her professional life in a way that values opportunities such as a research-based mentoring program? This question is not one easily answered with a simple affirmation. The search committee needs to probe candidates to find out when they have had similar experiences, ones where they worked closely with a senior colleague. We should also look for individuals whose confidence is so authentic that they are comfortable making mistakes and anxious to learn from them. There are many reasons for us to turn away from candidates with little evidence of self-reflection and poor communication skills since these limitations will have a negative impact upon many facets of their work. We need reflective leaders who see themselves as learners who are growing dynamically through engaging in their work. While aspiring administrators may claim to have these orientations, the Design Team holds that the board should seek specific evidence before it hires a new principal. It may sound simplistic, but the qualities of a successful protégé seem very much related to the qualities that will make this individual successful as an administrative leader in our district.

Preparing Mentors to Help New Principals

It is one thing to find potential mentors, and while this task seems daunting, it is only the first step. The leadership mentoring plan next needs to consider preparation of mentors to work effectively with protégés. Peel et al. (1998) highlight the need for the careful training of mentors. Mentors need to be advised that they face serious challenges (Crocker & Harris 2002) in simply assuming their role. They will be responsible for supporting, assisting, and guiding the process of the relationship as well as facilitating self-reliance in the protégé (Crocker & Harris 2002). Next, mentors must understand the richness of the task itself. Mentors will take on multiple roles, including that of a trusted colleague and developer who encourages (Head, Reiman, Thies, & Sprinthall 1992). While mentors are clearly role models, Restine (1993) points out that this is not a question of asking people to merely imitate an experienced veteran.

Next, mentors must be prepared to understand the relationship itself. One aspect of the connection between mentor and protégé is its complexity and the need for mutual trust and mutual valuing (Playko 1991). Establishing clear expectations and an expectation of confidentiality are key elements of this relationship (Dukess 2001). Mentors need to be sensitive to the depth of that relationship while not forgetting that this is also a professional association. Mentor and protégé are also engaged in an evolving partnership by the very nature of the work. Of course, one expects that the protégé will grow as a result of the support of the mentor's guidance. That is the primary purpose of the idea in the first place. This growth means that the kind of help needed by the protégé will change with time if the program is working as planned. The mentor also must understand that the protégé will grow in independence and honor this development.

Considering the maturation of the protégé is only one side of the equation. There is the growth of the mentor to consider as well, because this relationship is an important professional development for them as well (Cordeiro & Smith-Sloan 1995). Being committed to mentoring, giving help to a new generation of leaders, and sharing expertise so consistently will very likely lead to changes in self-image and raise the need to gain a broader perspective. A leadership mentoring program of high quality should include plans for the development of mentors into increasing levels of responsibility as they evolve.

Learning to Become an Effective Mentor

Selecting potentially gifted mentors and preparing them to have the right approach with protégés is a critical step leading logically to the question of content and process in the mentoring relationship. Simply put, what will the learning agenda be for protégés? If we look at this issue in the way we do with other learning experiences, three questions emerge. First, what will the learning agenda be? Normally, we refer to this as the curriculum. The next question is, how will we share the content with learners? This is another way to describe instruction. Finally, how will learners share what they have learned? Of course, this is an issue of assessment. These three elements have been used to describe the work of innovating schools in the United States and Canada (Gross 1998) where it was shown that a change in one of these elements would lead to a change in the other two. For instance, by expanding the curriculum to include local history, changes in instruction and assessment would quickly follow from the older approach of lecturing and testing. While this may initially look a little awkward because it is more typically found in discussions about learning experiences designed for our students, it is useful for our purposes since it helps us to organize the leadership mentoring program in a way that covers all three issues: What content matters? How will we share that content? How will we know that the protégé has learned the content?

The literature on mentoring programs shows that the work between mentor and protégé normally occurs through dialogues. These are not simple talking sessions but ones that are well organized and thoughtfully conducted (Barnett 1991). In these discussions, the mentor needs to help the protégé strike a balance between the natural need of the new principal to gain control of vital technical information and the requirement of school leaders to build a rich understanding of the larger picture of their school and education in general (Lashway 2003). New principals will fail if they have a poor understanding of how their district's budgeting system works, for instance. Yet, they will also fail to live up to their role as true educational leaders if they have no conception of national educational policy and its transformation over recent history or the need to make well-reasoned ethical decisions. One way for mentors to understand the problem of balancing the dialogues with protégés is to ask them to recall models of development such as Maslow's hierarchy of needs (1970). It could be said that the need for new principals to get a handle on the concrete parts of their job is closely related to the lower end of the hierarchy where people focus on survival. Will the principal get through the day successfully? Only after understanding the needs of the protégés as they evolve can the successful mentor guide the protégé to more abstract, yet equally vital, topics. This does not necessarily mean that a linear model of learning needs to be followed whereby new principals only focus on the technical side of their work to the exclusion of larger issues. It may be that the Design Team will suggest a blending-in of those topics from the start but in proportion to the ability of the new principal to grasp them comfortably.

Moving from this overview, we can turn to the kinds of content that the literature suggests for leadership mentoring programs. One promising plan describes four areas of technical learning for the protégé that seem appropriate for the early stages of the program:

- Daily operations
- Information collection, problem-solving strategies for these tasks
- Ways to work with a variety of adults
- Time management in the face of multiple tasks (Cordeiro & Smith-Sloan 1995)

Bolman and Deal (1993) use the case study of a new principal's first year and his reflections with a mentor to highlight five major lessons important to new principals:

- Mapping the school's politics
- Empowering people

- Aligning the structure with the job at hand
- Celebrating the school's culture
- Reframing using a variety of perspectives to understand a problem

If these four areas are reasonable parts of the early learning agenda or curriculum, others have depicted ways of sharing the agenda. Again, there are four steps:

- Teach them how.
- Let them do.
- Help them learn from having done.
- Accept them unconditionally.

Kay (1992 from Crocker & Harris 2002) speaks of training to deliver a four-step strategy.

This four-step strategy is a way of thinking through instruction between mentor and protégé with the last step; accepting the protégé unconditionally implies elements of assessment since acceptance follows the results of the protégé learning new tasks. Acceptance of the protégé does not imply ignoring problems since clear feedback is essential to the task of mentoring. It means valuing the person regardless of results.

A third model (Cordeiro & Smith-Sloan 1995) describing the development of protégé learning goes further than the ideas above since it takes mentoring from the early days when new principals typically have a limited grasp of the job to a much later stage when they have high "self and cultural awareness" (27–31):

- Initial contact (formal relationship; intern is still a stranger)
- Liminal stage (stress of the job really begins, protégé is diving into the work)
- Settling-in stage ("reflecting with mentors, scaffolding of tasks, and knowing there is a safety net")

- Efficacy stage (more autonomy for intern, creativity. "Interns consider themselves to be full members of their community.")
- Interdependence stage (great mutual benefits seen; thoughts of leaving are stressful)

Gross and Shapiro (2004) demonstrate the relevance of multiple ethical paradigms (including the ethics of justice, care, critique, and the profession) combined with turbulence theory (including the four levels of light, moderate, severe, and extreme) in a multiyear mentoring program. Through these allied approaches the mentor and protégé were able to address and respond to challenging ethical dilemmas.

As the Design Team builds a specific program of curriculum, instruction, and assessment for leadership mentoring in our district, we will come back to these guiding ideas since they provide a touchstone for our understanding of the key perspectives, approaches, and content areas we need to incorporate into our plan.

Matching of Mentors and Protégés

We believe that it is possible to identify seasoned educators with the potential to be superb mentors. It is also likely that we can help them learn effective approaches and specific content to share with protégés. We must also face the more tangible work of bringing mentors and protégés together.

While some districts opt for an assigned mentoring program, such a process seems inadequate to the task of forging meaningful relationships. If we hold to the standards set in the literature for a leadership mentoring program worthy of the name, we must be highly sensitive to this as a long-range, career-changing process for both the mentor and the protégé.

Equally important, we must be aware of potential difficulties described by scholars in this field. Geography may be a problem. Lashway (2003) speaks of the special problem of rural school districts, where a lack of money and personnel may make the matching process more difficult. But geography is not a possible barrier only for rural districts. Large cities have their own limiting factors of distance and financial limits, as do many large suburban districts. Yet, creative planners can find ways to transcend these constraints. In the opinion of the Design Team, it is a question of priorities. If we are determined to make the quality of the relationship our chief concern rather than apparent convenience, we will learn ways to create the most promising pairs of mentors and protégés.

A more daunting challenge facing us in matching mentors to protégés is the question of gender and racial balance. Currently, 60% of school principals are white males, 35% are females. Only 13% of school principals are men and women from racial minorities (Malone 2001). Finding sufficient female role models has been a longstanding problem. Pavan (1986) examined mentoring relationships in Pennsylvania schools and school districts. Among her findings was importance of mentoring aspiring female leaders, the lack of female mentors, and the fact that psychosocial functions (such as support and encouragement) were seen as most helpful. Matters (1994) describes a mentoring program in Australia designed to encourage more women to become school leaders. Difficulty in finding female mentors and the brevity of the program (two weeks of mentoring) were listed as problems to overcome. The Principals' Institute (Bank Street College) had as its focus increasing the number of women and minorities in leadership positions in public schools. Mentoring in this program lasted one semester and was considered to be the project's most useful aspect. Feedback from participants indicated that this preservice model would have been more useful if the mentoring relationship had been sustained for a longer period. Cohn and Sweeny (1992) connect the role of school districts in establishing effective mentoring programs, especially in helping underrepresented groups such as women and minorities in becoming principals.

Filling out the picture, there continues to be a high percentage of white males running the school system at the central office and on school boards. If we are committed to matching protégés with mentors who are of the same gender or same racial group and if we insist on creating mentors from among our own employees, we may not be able to create a viable system. Again, the Design Team believes that the standard of quality of relationship is vital. How similar do mentor and protégé need to be? This is a complex and highly sensitive question. While it is likely some of the pairs will not come from the same backgrounds, it is not inevitable that there will be vast differences in the perspective of the mentor and the protégé *if and only if* we are dedicated as well to the concept of true empathy and deep understanding on the part of the mentor. Obviously, this means a great deal of attention paid to the selection and education of mentors.

Time Requirements

Clearly, the creation of a promising leadership mentoring system requires attention to a range of issues that include abstract, ethical problem solving as well as concrete technical issues. In this way the plan itself mirrors the learning curve of the protégé, who also must blend learning specifics with gaining perspective on the larger issues facing education in our era. We are aware that some design qualities may at first appear to be simple technical issues that later are not so simple once we have thought about them a little more deeply. One such issue is time and the related concern of cost. How long should a mentoring program last? How much should it cost the district? We have finite resources of time and money and always will. We will also continue to have competing demands for both.

The literature suggests a great variety of models. Malone (2001) found varied lengths of the mentoring relationship from 165 hours to 632 hours. Dunavin (2004) found a multiyear program to be beneficial. "Evidence encouraged maintaining a structured mentor/coach relationship for the first three years of the new administrators' tenure. Further, as the mentoring progressed, a long-term model which incorporated evaluation promoted professional relationships in which learning goals were either achieved or re-negotiated" (Daresh 2001; Walker and Stott 1994; Wilmore 1995; Zachary 2000). Gross (2003) also described a multiyear program that resulted in a successful transition for a new high school principal.

Duration is only the most obvious aspect of the time issue. How often mentors and protégés are able to meet is just as important for planners to contemplate. Frequency has been a challenge for past programs. Barnett (1995) emphasizes the need for frequency as a key constant in program design. Crocker and Harris (2002) advocate for extra time to spend with protégés. Yet time itself needs to be focused. "Make specific guidelines available to mentors outlining activities and ways to involve mentees" (Crocker & Harris 2002).

In addition to our focus on helping new leaders in our midst, we also realize that our mentoring program may be aimed at helping our current assistant principals who aspire to become building leaders. Time potentials and constraints are equally important for this kind of mentor-protégé relationship. Paskey (1989) studied mentoring of assistant principals by their current principals and provides a general pattern for that relationship. Calabrese and Tucker-Ladd (1991) look at the kinds of issues that a mentoring principal should discuss with an assistant principal. They suggest that time each day needs to be taken to debrief and ask questions such as, "Why did you respond this way? What were the alternatives?" They also raise the question of separation. When and how should the mentoring relationship end? Crow and Matthews (1998) describe peer mentoring for mid-career leaders and discuss a year-long plan. Patience, understanding, and tolerance are among the required qualities for mentors, in their opinion.

CONCLUSION

The Design Team believes that this draft report fulfills the first charge given by the Randolph School Board because it responds to all four overarching questions:

1. There are clear problems facing principals in any era. However, today such issues as the national accountability movement and a generational change make the job of finding, nurturing, and keeping high-performing building leaders an especially challenging priority for almost every district.
2. Mentoring has a long and well-documented history from which we can learn. Clearly the relationship between an older, generative guide and a younger, maturing professional is found throughout history and has special relevance to our profession. Care, however, must be taken to ensure that these relationships are authentic and carry more than simply the name of mentoring.
3. Models of mentoring in North America and around the world also teach us that this is a pervasive phenomenon. Of equal importance, while there is variety in program design, certain patterns emerge, in program duration and learning content especially.
4. Good programs clearly place mentoring into the larger program of leadership induction. We suggest that great care be taken to expand the traditional meaning of the word "induction" into a more flexible, bidirectional process. Of equal significance, the literature tells us a great deal about the kinds of person who will make a good mentor as well as the types of person who will value the role of protégé. Mentorship education and the task of matching mentors to protégés is discussed in the literature. Here, the Design Team suggests sensitivity to matching women and underrepresented minorities with appropriate mentors. Clearly this is a subject we will need to address. Finally, the literature teaches us that larger programs, often extending to three years, are not only possible, they are encouraged.

While the Design Team does not believe that this report is the final word in leadership mentoring, we do conclude that this review gives us a well-reasoned and current foundation on which to make the next steps in program development. The literature provides guidance and general principles. We want to go further. In particular, the Design Team would like to build a program that uses the best of these ideas and also employs a central organizing theoretical framework on which to build leadership mentoring in our district.

CHAPTER 3

Mentoring, Ethical Decision Making, and Turbulence Theory: Keys to the Model of Leadership Mentoring

THE DESIGN TEAM TRIES A CREATIVE EXPERIMENT

Clearly, the first report had made a good impression on Betty and Antonio. With some minor feedback from them, the team members were prepared to make their first presentation to the school board and to the members of the public who were in attendance. The idea of starting out with a solid background in the area of mentoring in general and how it applied to nurturing new principals specifically proved to be a sound one. As one community member said during the question and answer period, "Well, this is the first time in a long while that I have seen some serious homework done when it comes time to plan a new program for the district. I had come here to listen to another report dealing with bus routes for the school year, but now I want to follow this mentoring program and see where it goes." A board member who worked as a mid-level executive added, "Good start. In our organization, we are used to seeing clear research behind new ideas. I am happy to see that you are taking the time to get it right before we start to spend even a little more money on this program. Of course, I understand that the cost of doing nothing is probably greater still. What I want to see is a continued use of solid evidence and the latest theories as we plan. Why shouldn't we have the best program around?" Betty and Antonio exchanged slight smiles at these responses. On the Design Team, Sam Grey and Ronnie Foldrona started to look just a bit proud of their work while the rest of the group were noticeably sitting a little taller in their seats. Walking out of the meeting, Ronnie turned to the team and said, "So far, so good. We have bought a little time and have built a little credibility.

Now comes the hard part, namely, following through." The Design Team understood its charge well and also understood that before long the members would be back at the next month's board meeting, where expectations were going to be higher. The board and the public would be looking for the same quality and the next step taking them closer to a sound leadership mentoring program.

Just two days later, the Design Team met for a working session, starting off with some remarks from Betty and Antonio. The superintendent and the board chair walked into the meeting room with a kind of quiet confidence. Their plan was starting to work. In a little over a month, the district had moved from simple awareness of a serious problem to a logical, engaging process of dealing with the looming crisis of losing new principals. They were allies in a cause that was far from won, but they were moving in what seemed increasingly the right direction. Betty smiled and opened the meeting. "Look, everyone, what happened at the board meeting is a great credit to you and your hard work in the first report. I know that you don't think the job is done or nearly done. But Antonio and I want you to appreciate that you're off to a fine start. I am not only speaking about the results, which are fine, but the process of working together seems to be paying off. Sam and Ronnie deserve a lot of credit for their leadership." Everyone in the room smiled and gave the pair a round of applause.

Antonio joined in. "Now that you have a foundation, what you need is a way of making choices from the research you have shared in the first report. Thanks to your writing, we understand the context for a leadership mentoring program. We have a clearer idea of the challenges facing new principals, the kinds of programs out there, the general history of mentoring, and the qualities we need to consider when selecting and educating mentors, as well as some elements that we will find in successful mentor-protégé relationships. As you have told us, and as the charge for the Design Team makes clear, you will have a chance later in the process to use these elements in the program design itself. Now, however, you have some selecting to do."

Zbigniew Lipecki was thinking along the same line. "Antonio is exactly right. We can't be all things to all people. In the first report, we were responsible to give ourselves, the board, and the community the widest possible range of reasonable perspectives. That was the foundation. Now, we need to stand for something, and that means making choices."

Something was bothering Sam Grey up to this point, and he saw an opening for his own perspective. "Well, I know that this is not the kind of research project that I normally work on, and I don't want to impose my own way of doing things, but the conversation is making me think about the charge we were given and the use of the next report to clarify things. We were asked to provide a context for leadership mentoring in the first report, and it seems that we did a reasonably good job. Now we are asked to think about the guiding theories we will use as the central element of our leadership mentoring program. So, that word *theory* is now part of our task."

Francine Beckwith rolled her eyes. "Look, we don't want to lose the public by sounding too, well, educationese. You know what happens when people start to speak in jargon; you make everyone feel like an outsider. They are paying for results, not a lot of high-sounding rhetoric."

Sam looked a little pained but continued, "Francine, this might surprise you, but I see things the same way. We are asked to be practical and we have been so far. I am not thinking about some convoluted set of ideas that will make people's eyes glaze over. What I am hoping for is something more of a gyroscope for the program. You see what I mean? Some clear organizing idea that will keep the program moving along and help us frame things."

Warren Bartman, the elementary school principal, saw a spark of hope in Sam's last statement. "As long as you are thinking about it in that way, I could agree with spending our time this month on a guiding theory. But how will we come up with something like that?"

Ronnie Foldrona was quick to point out the way to their next step. "I don't think we need to come up with a theory. That's not our job.

What we have so far is a host of ideas worked on by many people all around the world. What we need to be are thoughtful consumers. We need to look back over the last report and select the ideas that we feel could serve as the guiding theory. Our task is not one of inventing but one of identifying. This means that we need to agree on criteria for this theory and go about the task of coming to agreement."

As the conversation progressed and took on energy, Betty and Antonio quietly smiled and left the room. They understood that the Design Team had its own decisions to make and it would be best for the group to settle down and work in private. The upshot of the discussion, after some understandable rambling, was a set of workable ideas that would help the Design Team find the organizing theory on which to build its leadership mentoring program.

Ronnie took a stab at pulling the discussion together. "So, we seem to have something verging on consensus, or at least it sounds that way to me. Here is what I am hearing from the group. First, although there is a need for early mentoring to focus on mechanical and technical issues, the literature tells us that this will fade in most cases. So a set of ideas that keeps our attention on those issues will not carry us as far as we need the program to go. Next, we know that other problems, specifically those dealing with difficult decision making, are going to persist. These are also ones that seem to come with ethical dilemmas attached to them. Third, we know that the leadership mentoring program is a long-term proposition. We could have spared everyone a lot of effort and time by simply going for a cut-and-paste of someone else's two-month program if we wanted to be done with this. We have decided, as a community, to try a deeper approach. This means investing in the development of the mentor and the protégé as thinking educational professionals."

Ashley Roth's face lit up. "Right. I spend my time thinking about professional development and this follows all of the best advice I have found in the literature and at conferences. We need to be about educating for the long term, not narrow training, when we speak about something like a principal's ability to work through serious ethical dilemmas. This means that we must select a theory from the literature that helps with ethical decision making, helps deepen the dialogues between mentor and protégé, has the ability to last throughout much of the program's duration, and has the potential of greater professional learning for both mentor and protégé."

Sam, Zbigniew, Warren, Ronnie, and Francine were nodding. These were the criteria. "All right then," Sam seemed determined to push things forward. "If we agree with those as the crucial ideas for our leadership mentoring program, I have a nomination. I think that the concept of multiple ethical paradigms and turbulence theory written by Shapiro and Gross should be our guiding theoretical framework. These two perspectives focus on decision making, especially when principals are faced with ethical dilemmas. They also help leaders understand the level of unrest or turbulence in a given problem. They are structured in a way that could lead to rich conversations between mentor and protégé, and they represent a way of thinking through problems that can be learned. Finally, Gross and Shapiro have used this approach with their own students, who are typically administrators facing the same challenges as our own principals. So, we may be talking about theory, but it is the kind of theory that has ready application."

It was agreed that the combined ideas of the multiple ethical paradigms and turbulence theory would be the hook upon which the Design Team would hang much of their program. Other elements would be crucial for the leadership mentoring program to be effective, they all would concede. But these two ideas (now shortened to MEP/TT) would become a kind of touchstone for the bulk of their work.

With a theatrical clearing of her throat and a wry smile, Francine spoke up. "OK, you've sold me on the need for a theory in the first place and on this particular theory as the backbone of our leadership mentoring program. Fine. But, we need to remember something. We have worked together as a team, building up some trust in each other and some tolerance for ideas that are a bit strange to us because of that trust. We also have had the, well, privilege I suppose you'd call it, of spending time reading a good deal on this subject and getting comfortable with all of these ideas. This is great for our little group in this room today, but the people we are sharing our ideas with have had none of these experiences. We need to remember that when we go forward. How can we bring them into the making of this program, or at least not turn them off as we continue to meet our charge?"

Ashley and Zbigniew nodded. "Look, Francine is exactly right. We were selected because we represent important groups in the district, both of the professionals and from the community. Now that we are working on a theory, we are looking into something that may even frighten our neighbors." Zbigniew was speaking from his heart and convinced the group.

At this point, the members of Design Team took an unanticipated step. They decided that the time had come to really trust each other and the process of working together. If they were a highly functioning group, with a good track record so far, why not trust that they could work creatively? So, the brainstorming process began, leading rapidly to Ronnie's suggestion of a way to structure the next report, which blended the theoretical content with a compelling story.

As Warren later recalled, "My mind kept going back to a little history that I had read about Franklin Roosevelt's fireside chats and how FDR always pictured his neighbor, a farmer in Hyde Park, New York, sitting across from his desk. President Roosevelt aimed his talks at this farmer and his family, and the result was that he could communicate serious, sometimes complicated ideas with clarity and compassion. He never condescended to the people and he rarely confused them because he kept them clearly in mind as he spoke. We decided to do the same thing, but with a little twist. We kept our public in mind as we brainstormed and decided that the best way to introduce these theories was by telling a story. Alone, they may seem dry or a little out of reach. In the context of a story, however, they might come alive. We not only felt good about this approach, we felt a new energy. I can't find other words for it but to say that we were getting playful. The story started to come alive and we knew that we were on to something important." Just as Sam took primary responsibility for assembling the pieces of the first report, Ronnie agreed to be first author of the story that would bring the multiple ethical paradigms and turbulence theory onto center stage. "You know that I am a pretty confident building administrator," she smiled, "and not overly shy. But this is a little new to me. I'm not a fiction writer, but what I can do is to write up a story, based on a real experience, that I think will get us into the issue of ethical decision making, turbulence, and the mentor-protégé relationship. Then, maybe someone else, or some group, can build a bridge to the theories themselves. How does that sound?"

As a result, Ronnie and the group developed the story of Rudy Winthrop and his struggle with a profound ethical dilemma.

PRINCIPAL WINTHROP'S DILEMMA

Rudy Winthrop is a first-year principal who has taken over Wayne High School after a promising career as a chemistry teacher and then as an assistant principal in a neighboring district. Unfortunately, Wayne High's fall semester has gotten off to a rocky start for Rudy owing to a dispute between a popular English literature teacher and a group of parents. The teacher, Wanda Solander, started a new course this year whose focus was on American identity. Wanda challenged the notion that America needed to be a Eurocentric culture and stressed the need to think of our country as a world culture where no one culture held dominance.

This approach was popular with some students and quite unpopular with others. After failing one essay examination, a group of students met with their parents and decided to protest. Their focus was not on their grades per se; it was on the approach that Ms. Solander took. Parents questioned her judgment. "America is standing up to enemies all over the world," said the father of one student in an angry letter to Rudy. "This is no time to make our children confused about who they are and what their heritage is. I am not paying my taxes for that kind of propaganda!" Soon, letters to the editor of the local newspaper started to appear. Some families supported Ms. Solander and commended her broad-minded approach to curriculum. One couple wrote a letter that said in part, "In a world filled with anger and misunderstanding, our children need to take a broader view and deepen their perspective. They are not infants, and some of them may even see combat before too long. Our students need a brave teacher like Ms. Solander to help them see this emerging, complex world." Neither side was settling down and both threatened to take some kind of direct action, though just what that meant was unclear. One letter to Rudy ended this way, "Above all, we expect a leader in the principal's office, NOT A BUREAUCRAT. Which side are you on?"

Rudy knew that he would face many unforeseen issues when he took the keys to the principal's office and started his tenure as Wayne High's leader that past July. What he did not count on was this kind of controversy. He was confused since he did not know how he himself felt about this question. He had well-considered opinions on most of the more typical educational issues of the day—he knew where he stood on high-stakes testing, for example. But this was almost a national political question, and it also was one that looked as though it might quickly spin out of control. If left unattended, it could easily draw precious resources of time, energy, and money that Rudy and the whole district could use otherwise.

On the morning that Rudy was scheduled to have his monthly meeting with the district superintendent, Dr. Evelyn Krenst, his anxiety was ratcheted up a notch. Ms. Solander had received a threatening phone call at her home and called the police. She also demanded that Rudy do something to protect her at once or she would file a lawsuit against him and the district.

Rudy decided that before he met with Superintendent Krenst at the district office, he would call his mentor, Samantha Delano.

Samantha agreed that the situation was serious and that Rudy was wise to seek support. They agreed to meet that morning, prior to his meeting with Dr. Krenst. Just before hanging up, Samantha left Rudy with this thought: "Look, this is not an easy one, I know you see that. Before we meet, maybe you should take a walk and ask yourself a couple of questions. First, how serious is this situation, for whom, and how do you know? Second, how will you decide what is right in this situation for you, the students, their families, and Ms. Solander? Don't worry so much about a solution for now; just spend time thinking about how you will think about this. We'll take it from there once we meet, OK?"

Rudy had worked for months with Samantha and understood that most of her mentoring started off in this fashion. While a little part of him wanted a simple solution and a cookbook recipe for this problem, his more mature side realized that an issue looming as large as this one was unlikely to admit of an easy answer. "I think I understand your point. I'll see you soon." With that, Rudy walked down the corridor leading to the front door, walked out, and suddenly became lost in thought.

Rudy Winthrop faced a complex and potentially volatile problem that could not be ignored. It included teachers, parents, community members, and students. It was value laden, politically charged, and just the sort of thing that draws headlines. Educational leadership is never the place for simplistic responses, and this case demonstrates that fact very well. Samantha Delano's questions for Rudy focused on how he should approach his own thinking about this problem. How might he take her advice and not become lost in endless reflection just at a time when he needs to take action?

Taking a Systematic Approach

Being able to look at things in much of their complexity without becoming swamped with information requires a systematic approach. In this case, there are two kinds of thinking needed before deciding on a course of action. First, Rudy needs to understand the level of severity that this problem represents. Is this a full-blown crisis? Looked at differently, is this an issue that can be delegated to a support person or a committee? Is the situation lost? The answer to this question will help Rudy and anyone working with him decide on the priority that this problem will take in the long line of other pressing issues facing any school principal. To help Rudy reflect on this aspect of a dilemma, Samantha introduced him to something called turbulence theory, which will be described below.

Following a clear understanding of the severity of a given dilemma, Rudy will need to consider the kind of ethical lens that he will use when charting a serious response. Again, Samantha had taught him that ethics is far richer and more complex than simply reading a manual on proper administrative behavior and obeying its precepts. The field is one that combines multiple perspectives, or paradigms, that leaders need to consider as they reflect upon their options. These ethical lenses will also be outlined below.

Finally, after trying to fathom the priority that this issue deserves and weighing the kinds of ethical lenses that he can use to understand the problem and make a decision, Rudy will return to turbulence theory once again. This time, the question concerns his best estimate of the effect that his actions will have on the turbulence surrounding this issue. Not only that, he needs to consider who might experience what degree of turbulence and make appropriate accommodations.

It is the combination of turbulence theory dynamically blended with multiple ethical paradigms that Samantha used in helping Rudy move from a gut-level response to ethical decision making to a logical, systematic approach. Through their mentor-protégé relationship, she helped him to grasp the theories clearly, then to apply them to cases in selected texts, and finally to use this system so regularly that it became habit of mind. Once this way of thinking was in place, it became a kind of disposition for them both and a centerpiece of their dialogues.

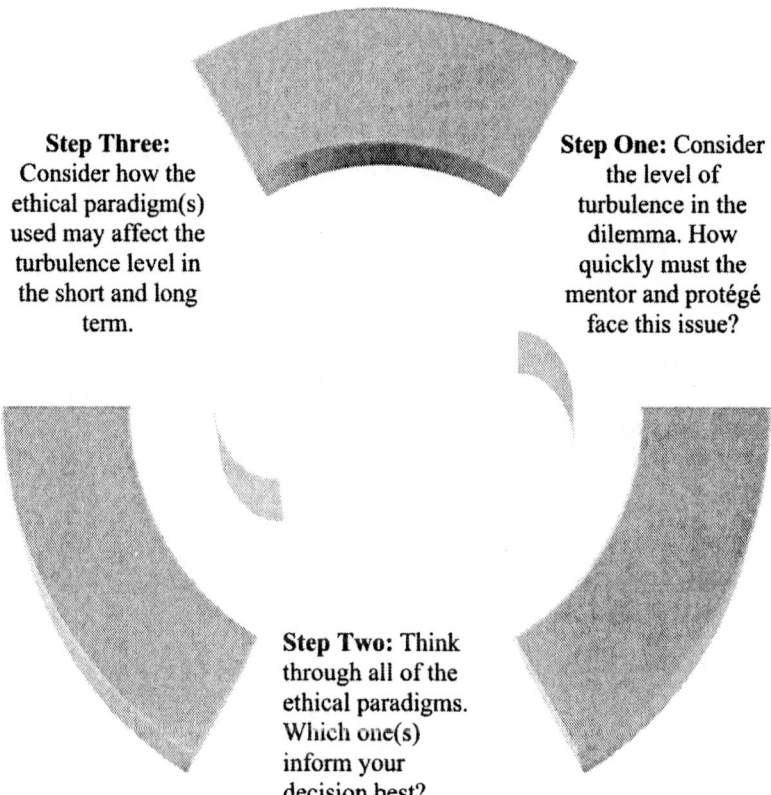

Figure 3.1. Using Multiple Ethical Paradigms and Turbulence Theory as an Integrated System

A BRIEF INTRODUCTION TO TURBULENCE THEORY

In his book *Staying Centered: Curriculum Leadership in a Turbulent Era*, Gross (1998) found that sites that had developed curriculum, instructional, and assessment innovations for several years all experienced some degree of turbulence or volatile conditions. Further, he discovered that the degree of turbulence at the 10 schools and districts he had studied could be divided into four levels, as follows.*

---

*"A Brief Introduction to Turbulence Theory" and "A Brief Introduction to the Multiple Paradigms Approach to Ethics" appear in Gross and Shapiro (2004). Reprinted with permission.

Light turbulence includes ongoing issues with the normal functioning of the school. Examples of this include dealing with a disjointed community or geographic isolation of the school. One school responded to its geographic isolation by joining a national reform organization and by hosting an annual statewide conference on innovation at small schools. The key to light turbulence is the fact that it is part of the school's environment and that it can be handled easily in a way that will at least keep the issue in check.

Moderate turbulence is related to specific issues that are widely recognized as important and needing to be solved. The loss of an important support structure would be one example of moderate turbulence. Rapid growth of the student body would be another. One school, faced with the sudden expansion in the number of students, made this issue the center of in-service meetings just prior to the opening of school. Faculty were trained in ways to welcome, listen to, and integrate new students. The principal modeled the attitude of acceptance by stating that the new students were not simply joining their school but also had every right to help change the school since that fit the school's philosophy. Moderate turbulence, therefore, is not part of normal operations, it quickly gains nearly everyone's attention, and yet it can be responded to with a focused effort.

Severe turbulence is found in cases where the whole enterprise seems threatened. A conflict of community values was at the heart of one instance of severe turbulence in Gross's study. In that case, members of the community were deeply divided in their reaction to specific reforms. School board elections became highly emotional, friendships were ended because of pressure to join one faction or another, and the process of reform was suspended. The district used a four-stage strategy to respond to this dilemma. This included shifting to issues upon which agreement was more easily reached, electing a centrist community member to serve as board chair, holding televised meetings of a strategic planning council, and reminding community members that stability and trust rather than disharmony were the district's norms. In severe turbulence the problems are so serious that normal administrative actions seem inadequate. A coor-

Table 3.1. Degree and General Definitions of Turbulence Found in Educational Settings

Degree of Turbulence	General Definition
Light	Associated with ongoing issues, little or no disruption in normal work environment, subtle signs of stress
Moderate	Widespread awareness of the issue, specific origins
Severe	Fear for the entire enterprise, possibility of large-scale community demonstrations, a feeling of crisis
Extreme	Structural damage to the school's normal operation is occurring. Collapse of the reform seems likely.

dinated set of strategies is very likely needed, while business-as-usual thinking needs to be suspended.

Extreme turbulence involves serious danger of the destruction of the institution. Gross speculated that this degree of turbulence was possible, based on the fact that institutions do, of course, become unraveled. All of the 10 sites in the 1998 study were able to respond to their own cases of turbulence, ranging from light to severe, with success. A follow-up study (Gross 2000) did reveal a case of extreme turbulence where a cascading series of pressures caused an end to the entire reform process.

Turbulence theory therefore gives us an enhanced ability to calibrate the severity of the issue at hand. It further aids us in our attempt to contextualize a given problem as we construct strategies to move to less troubled waters.

A BRIEF INTRODUCTION TO THE MULTIPLE PARADIGMS APPROACH TO ETHICS

The underlying perspectives for helping educational leaders solve dilemmas in turbulent times are provided in a book entitled *Ethical Leadership and Decision Making in Education: Applying Theoretical Perspectives to Complex Dilemmas*. This work, written by Shapiro and Stefkovich (2001), takes into account the four ethical paradigms of justice, critique, care, and the profession. Starratt (1994) had brought together three of the paradigms in his approach to ethics and schools but this model added the fourth lens, the perspective of the profession.

The ethic of justice focuses on rights and law and is part of a liberal democratic tradition that, according to Delgado (1995), "is characterized by incrementalism, faith in the legal system, and hope for progress" (1). The liberal part of this tradition is defined as a "commitment to human freedom," and the democratic aspect implies "procedures for making decisions that respect the equal sovereignty of the people" (Strike 1991, 415). Contemporary ethical writings in education using the foundational principle of the ethic of justice include, among others, works by Kohlberg (1981), Beauchamp and Childress (1984), Strike, Haller, and Soltis (1988), Goodlad, Soder, and Sirotnik (1990), and Sergiovanni (1992).

The ethic of critique has been discussed by a number of writers and activists (e.g., Apple 1988; Bakhtin 1981; Bowles & Gintis 1988; Freire 1970; Foucault 1983; Giroux 1994; Greene 1988; Purpel & Shapiro 1995) who are not convinced by the analytic and rational approach of the justice paradigm. Some of these scholars find a tension between the ethic of justice, rights, and laws and the concept of democracy. Not only do they force us to rethink important concepts such as democracy, but they also ask us to redefine and reframe other concepts such as privilege, power, culture, language, and even justice. This ethic asks educators to deal with the hard questions regarding social class, race, gender, and other areas of difference, such as, Who makes the laws? Who benefits from the law, rule, or policy? Who has the power? Who are the silenced voices?

The ethic of care has been articulated by some feminist scholars (e.g., Beck 1994; Belenky, Clinchy, Goldberger, & Tarule 1986; Gilligan 1982; Gilligan, Ward, & Taylor 1988; Noddings 1984/1992; Shapiro & Smith-Rosenberg 1989) who have challenged this dominant, and what they consider to be often patriarchal, ethic of justice in our society by turning to the ethic of care for moral decision making. Attention to this ethic can lead to other discussions of concepts such as loyalty, trust, and empowerment. This ethic asks that individuals consider the consequences of their decisions and actions. It asks them to consider questions such as, Who will benefit from what I decide? Who will be hurt by my actions? What are the long-term effects of a decision I make today? And if I am helped by someone now, what should I do in the future about giving back to this individual or to society in general?

Finally, the ethic of the profession has been developed most recently in a 1996 document, *Standards for School Leaders* (ISLLC, 1996). Of these, standard 5 states: "A school administrator is an educational leader who promotes the success of all students by acting with integrity, fairness, and in an ethical manner" (ISLLC 1996, 18). In creating their ethic of the profession paradigm, Shapiro and Stefkovich (2001) placed the best interests of the student at the center. Additionally, a number of education-related professional organizations have developed their own professional ethical codes. Some of these ethical codes are relatively new and others are long-standing. Examples of these organizations include, but are certainly not limited to, the American Association of School Administrators, the American Association of University Professors, the American Psychological Association, the Association of School Business Officials, the Association for Supervision and Curriculum Development, and the National Education Association. While the term "ethics" is used in the United States, "values" also has been mentioned, particularly in Canada, as the term used in relationship to the profession of educational administration (Begley 1999).

RUDY APPLIES MEP/TT TO THIS SITUATION THROUGH A DIALOGUE WITH SAMANTHA

Rudy reflected on the general qualities of turbulence theory and multiple ethical paradigms as a first step. Then, he went to work applying these combined ideas as he prepared to meet with Samantha. As was their practice, Samantha asked Rudy to describe his analysis as she thought the situation over with him, helping him to raise and answer questions.

"Samantha, this is a tough one, and I am very glad that we have some kind of organized way to work through this issue. If it is not handled well, this problem could damage a lot of people and maybe end a career or two. I have some serious worries, and I need to share my thinking with you. Are you ready?"

"Rudy, it's much easier for me in one way and harder in another. You are living it; I am only seeing it through your eyes. The impact will hit me indirectly, but I am very concerned, because it does seem like a rough situation. Let's take this one step at a time and see how you organized your thinking, OK?"

"Right, here goes. First, I went back to the fundamentals of turbulence theory to estimate how serious things were. As we have done with earlier problems, I made a turbulence gauge. Again, as in our earlier discussions, I started by considering the four levels of turbulence and their general definitions.

"It's my guess that we are in severe turbulence already since there is community unrest, a belief that there will be demonstrations of some kind and already an air of crisis. That led me to construct a turbulence gauge for this specific situation. I started that by filling in the 'severe' level first. That was easy since I know what conditions exist and feel strongly that they are severe. Next, I filled in the other three levels. The 'extreme' level was not hard since it represents my fears, or where things could go if the problem gets more out of our control. The 'moderate' level is where I would like us to go next since I am not sure that we can take the leap from where we are now to light turbulence. I took my time to define light turbulence because I did not want to be naïve or unrealistic. A course that calls attention to America's values taught with passion when we have soldiers far away is unlikely to be overlooked. I described light turbulence in this situation with that in mind. Here is my tentative turbulence gauge." (See Table 3.2.)

Samantha was impressed. "Rudy, you really have a handle on building turbulence gauges! From your work and the way you have described the situation, I agree, it is severe with every potential of becoming extreme. We could say that our challenge is to help you

Table 3.2. Turbulence Gauge for Wayne High School's Dilemma

Degree of Turbulence	General Definition	Applied to this Situation
Light	Associated with ongoing issues; little or no disruption in normal work environment; subtle signs of stress	The course becomes valued because it is serious and challenging. The teacher works for balance without becoming bland. Communication is high among school, home, and family.
Moderate	Widespread awareness of the issue; specific origins	Serious dialogue occurs among all parties. Perspectives are shared, but there is still a sense that the course needs development. Mutual respect prevails.
Severe	Fear for the entire enterprise; possibility of large-scale community demonstrations; a feeling of crisis	Angry parents complain. Forced choice with a lose-lose potential. Teacher the target of hatred. Problem starting to boil over. Will central office support the principal?
Extreme	Structural damage to the school's normal operation is occurring. Collapse of the reform seems likely.	Steady, volcanic pressure forces the teacher to resign; pressure on the principal is likewise intense. Central office walks away, leaving the community split and angry. A legacy of contempt is woven into the school's fabric. Future innovations of this kind seem highly unlikely.

find a strategy to bring this down to a moderate level for now. Before you go on to the multiple ethical paradigm view of things, do you have any other thoughts on turbulence?"

"Well, there are three other points related to turbulence theory that we should include. First, there is something called *cascading*. In general, cascading happens when the turbulence from one event blends with another to create a higher level of turbulence. For our case, this could easily happen because our district is about to attempt to pass its budget. Emotions from the increased taxes that may result from the new budget could readily link to the feeling surrounding this course, resulting in an escalation. Just as easily, if we experience violence against the United States here or abroad, supporters of the course and its critics could easily raise their emotional level.

"After cascading, there is the issue of *turbulence as a positive force* (Gryskiewicz 1999). While I'm up at nights worrying about where this could go as a problem, hurting innocent people, I also need to remember that a course like this, taught by a reasonable and pretty courageous teacher, is something to be proud of. If we work carefully on this problem, we could pave the way for other courses that really touch students at a deep level. This is certainly a teachable moment, as the textbooks would say.

"Finally, turbulence theory requires me to remember *positionality*. Positionality is the concept that everyone in the organization does not experience the same level of turbulence at the same time. It is not usually spread around the school and community in a uniform way. In our case, the teacher is under the community's microscope; she is probably at least at severe turbulence. Additionally, the students and their parents are going to feel pressured. What if a student likes the course and comes home to an angry pair of parents every night? What if the student hates the course and must come to class every day and experience what to her is a hostile environment? The central office is feeling lots of tension, and, of course, so am I."

Samantha was becoming very proud of her protégé and his ability to step back from a looming crisis to gather evidence. "You are doing a wonderful job, Rudy. I would add only one thing that we need to keep in mind. In spite of everything swirling around us, you have to remember, and you have to remind others, that turbulence is nothing unnatural. Just the opposite. It is a fundamental aspect of our world and of the whole universe. Things are moving at all times and at all levels, in an organism or an organization like yours. That movement, that turbulence, is nothing we should want to escape, but something to understand and try to use. That is probably the most important aspect of turbulence for us to consider. With your work on turbulence theory you also blended in the ideas of multiple ethical paradigms. Where did that work take you?"

"Taking time to look through each of the ethical paradigms helped me to weigh alternatives and it kept me from rushing things," Rudy replied. "From our talks and from my own experience, I know that we are tempted to rely heavily on the ethic of justice, so I will start off with that. However, I want you to know that I understand there is a bias toward using the ethic of justice too much, and I've tried to balance my thinking.

"Looked at from the ethic of justice perspective, my first question is, What does the law say? What rules are there and have they been followed? This is a great example of how this ethic may not take us very far in thinking over a dilemma such as this one. Rules? Well, for one thing, I checked on the rules for starting a new course. Our teacher went through all of the formal steps and presented the course outline, materials to be used, and lesson plans. To my best knowledge, she has followed them to the letter. I also checked on our union contract. She has done nothing that is outside of the contract, so she is in the clear there as well. At a higher level, there is the issue of her rights to academic freedom. This is a little gray, and I have not had the chance to look into case law on this subject. However, if academic freedom means anything, it should allow a teacher to present even a controversial subject in her field as long as there is some attempt at balance. She has done this.

"So, if I were to rely solely upon the ethic of justice, I am not sure what I would say to angry parents and community members. No rule has been violated. But what am I supposed to do? Tell them to mind their own business when I also know that the ethic of justice tells me that the law requires that their children attend school and, thereby, be exposed to ideas and an approach that they reject?

"That led me to the ethic of care. Here, I needed to consider some questions such as, Who will benefit from what I decide? Who will be hurt by my actions? What are the long-term effects of a decision I make today? And if I am helped by someone now, what should I do in the future about giving back to this individual or to society in general? The answers were kind of revealing. If we stop the class, for instance, some parents will be happy with us. Others will be hurt. The same thing with students. Even if the majority will be happy, does that make it right? On a larger scale, what will this do to any future attempts to try an innovation? If I reversed the possible course of action and simply held my ground, what message does that send to the community? Do I want the school and my leadership to be characterized by stonewalling when we get criticized? So, the ethic of care did help me because it showed me that any extreme position would probably backfire in the future or even in the short run.

"That brought me to the ethic of critique. This is powerful and challenging since it caused me to wonder, Who makes the laws? Who benefits from the law, rule, or policy? Who has the power? And who are the silenced voices? The fact is, families have a little say when it comes to school curriculum since we do have a school board and the board has a curriculum committee. However, that is not very helpful to most community members. I mean, what noneducator can wade through all of the paperwork and understand things like state standards, benchmarks, adequate yearly progress, and all of that rhetoric? So, the law kind of places so-called experts in a powerful position. Maybe we deserve that trust, but in a situation like this, obviously, that is not what everyone thinks. The ethic of critique can be used when we think over the content of the course itself. Here we have a teacher who is willing to challenge the positions of the most powerful people in the society. She is giving students a different perspective from the one most of the media provides, and she does a good job of bringing in many points of view. This is not really a case of a teacher on a soapbox, despite what everyone on the other side thinks. I value the courage of this teacher and the ethic of critique shows me why. Yet, that same ethic tells me that we need to be mindful of the lack of power that the dissenting parents feel. It is legitimate as well. Again, I am left with the strong feeling that one-sided responses will not serve us.

"That leaves the ethic of the profession. Here, I wondered what our responsibilities were as professional educators. The literature is a little new in this area and writers like Shapiro and Stefkovich (2001) have made a point that in the ethic of the profession, it is the interest of students that comes first. They are in the center. I thought about that a good deal. What does it mean to place students at the center? Doesn't everyone claim to do just that? Don't both sides of this dispute feel that they are fighting on behalf of students? But that is only a surface perspective. Our profession speaks about lifelong learning and preparation for living in a democratic society. Those may sound like catchphrases to some people, but if we don't take them seriously, who will? That led me to conclude that this course is important to our students' understanding of our country and the role it does and will play in the world. No question about it. If I want to use the ethic of the profession as my lens, I have to hold on to that. If we give up on this course, we will be doing students a disservice. Yet, if we don't deal with the controversy surrounding it effectively, it will be taken away from us. No doubt about that either."

Samantha knew that it was her turn to help Rudy pull the pieces together. "Let me see if I can summarize a little before we start to consider any action for you to suggest to the superintendent. First, the turbulence level is severe with the possibility of getting to the extreme stage if we are not careful. It is especially turbulent for the teacher in question and some of the students. With other issues around the district such as the budget, there is the possibility that turbulence will get worse no matter what we do, but that should not stop us from coming up with a proposal designed to lower the level from severe to moderate. Your turbulence gauge will help everyone understand what you mean by moderate.

"Next, your summary of the four ethical lenses makes it clear that this is truly an ethical dilemma with no easy answer. Listening to you, I was struck by the way you used the ethic of the profession to support this course. Clearly, from what you've said, the solution must include keeping the course. But your use of the ethic of critique and the ethic of care shows that there must be room for parents and community members to feel heard and possibly participate in some way. Is there a way for the course to include their input without surrendering the academic freedom of the teacher and thereby setting a terrible precedent?"

"I was afraid that you would end up there because I was headed there as well," Rudy said. "The trouble with our thinking is that it could be handled poorly and simply look like we were caving in to pressure. If we are going to have community involvement at the course-design level, it is going to have to be very carefully developed, with clear guidelines. We don't want to empower just anyone to be a kind of intellectual gatekeeper. On the other hand, these are the public's schools and there should be a role for the public."

From this opening conversation, the two went on to outline some steps that Rudy could bring to the superintendent. The board's curriculum committee could be expanded to include parents who supported and those who were against this course. Meetings with parents and students could be facilitated so that everyone could be heard. Here, accurate information could be shared so that everyone would be using facts, not rumors, when speaking about the course. In the extreme case of a family objecting to the course despite all of these efforts, students could be given an alternative assignment, but there would have to be a clear policy surrounding this suggestion. Finally, Samantha and Rudy looked at the emerging strategy and at Rudy's turbulence gauge, asking themselves the central question: If these solutions were put into place, would they reflect the ethics that Rudy used, and would they likely lead to a reduction of turbulence to the moderate level?

"Samantha, here's what I said would amount to moderate turbulence: 'Serious dialogue occurs between all parties. Perspectives are shared but there is still a sense that the course needs development. Mutual respect does prevail.' I don't know how you are feeling, but to me, that describes our approach pretty well. We are supporting ideas that will lead to dialogue, that are inclusive, and that will probably help the course to improve with time. Also, what we are supporting will give the course its best chance of meeting students' needs. Of course, we can't be sure that this will work, but I do feel a whole lot more confident about my meeting with the superintendent. I can stand behind this approach."

Clearly, the Design Team worked hard to understand and apply the lessons of multiple ethical paradigms and turbulence theory. They were, however, just a bit nervous when it came time to share this part of their charge with the school board and Betty.

Warren was the first to admit his trepidations to the rest of his group. "Look, I understand what we did and am very impressed with our work, if that is not being too immodest. But we have to remember that normal school board meetings are not typically the place for creativity. We may get criticized, and I don't want any of you disappointed if that happens."

He and the others were a little surprised when the otherwise self-contained Zbigniew Lipecki spoke up with passion. "At the start of this phase, I told you that we had to make some choices. Well, that was true for selecting a theory to share, and it is true for the way we are sharing that theory. Warren is right; we could have done things differently, but in an atmosphere of change, what was once tried and true now may simply be tired and through! We not only selected a theory, we showed how it worked in a really tough situation *and we showed how it worked in the context of a mentor-protégé relationship through dialogue.* I say we go in with confidence in our work and in each other, be prepared for some clarifying questions, and get ready to think about the follow-up meetings."

With that attitude, the Design Team shared its theoretical perspective with the superintendent, the school board, and the public. Zbigniew was quite accurate in his prediction; there was general understanding of the ideas in this report and more than one congratulations from the board. The sentiment was one of pride that this school district and its Design Team were able to fathom some late-breaking theories and apply them to the leadership mentoring process.

Antonio was among many who felt that the district was on its way to a successful plan with high standards. "You know what? We are going from being way behind others on this issue to becoming something of a trendsetter. I am not talking about a fad but about showing ourselves and our public that we are going to have a program that asks a lot of everyone and delivers the same. People who want to become mentors with this level of sophistication will need to be very well educated indeed. If I have a caveat for the Design Team to match my appreciation for their work, it is that very point. We need to make sure that we plan for the type of learning for mentors that will lead them to success. That will make for some wonderful professional development."

CHAPTER 4

The Design Team Faces a New Hurdle: Time to Keep It Real

Looking back, most people on the Design Team would say that the eureka moment came from a remark made by Francine Beckwith, the parent and community member of the group, at the meeting following their board presentation. The group was gaining confidence after its second public meeting went well. Not everyone in the group was certain that theory was the way to go, but the smiles at the board meeting and the e-mail that came from members of the public added to the sense of being on the right track. It was getting almost too comfortable.

Then Francine changed the situation. "I think I am going to quit the Design Team!" The odd thing was not so much her statement but the quizzical smile on her face. Francine was hardly angry, she was simply filled with wonder as she explained her rather remarkable statement. "I guess I've shocked you. That wasn't what I wanted to do. But look. The direction is great, we have made lots of progress, and I think that you are going to be able to complete the charge nearly on time. I am thrilled with the way we are working and I like all of you—even you, Zbig! But I had a goal for myself when I decided to join the Design Team, and that is what is getting hard to see happen anymore. I wanted two things out of the process: to contribute on par with the rest of you and to learn on par as well. I have certainly learned a great deal. That is not it. I don't feel that I am contributing, and I want to feel that I am doing my share. The reason I kind of smiled when I told you that I am likely to resign is that I never, repeat *never* expected to say that I want to leave a group because I needed to have more work!"

This chapter was coauthored with Joan Poliner Shapiro.

With that, the others gave a mild laugh. Sam made the first attempt to reply. "Francine, I hope that you think about it some more before you make up your mind. Yes, we have had two good reports and the board seems happy. But we have a long way to go. In fact, I wanted to speak with the group about that today. We did lay a foundation with the first report, and we showed that we had priorities in theory with the second report. But did you see the look on everyone's face when Ms. Burg spoke about a real-life example? It was as if she threw a switch connecting everyone in the room; they all seemed to jump a little and agree. The charge for the next section is also aimed at that. Well, connecting that to Francine's concern about contributing, I have a suggestion. What if we consider the literature once more and this time find a case study that most closely connects with our sense of what a leadership mentoring program needs to do? And, what if we change our process just a bit and give the organizing task to Francine and me? It is a bit like the work we did in considering the literature in the first report, because it is the kind of work that I do every semester. But if Francine joins me in this, she can certainly make a strong contribution and it may be a good learning experience. Francine, what do you think?"

And so a new direction and a work team were established. This time, there would be an experienced researcher pairing up with a novice. That meant that the Design Team itself was starting to build some mentoring into its own work or, to use the phrase that had become Ronnie Foldrona's trademark, they were starting to walk the walk.

The goal for this aspect of the work was to provide a real context for leadership mentoring. What does this kind of relationship look like in practice? Sam and Francine quickly realized that there might not be a case that was a perfect example of what they wanted. However, as they pored over the literature, they felt confident that they could find a case that had many of the general qualities that they wanted the community to see. Since the example that they used in the previous report detailing multiple ethical paradigms and turbulence theory was hypothetical, they were intent on documenting a real-life situation.

Sam, Francine, and Ashley Roth, who decided to join the subgroup, were almost buried underneath a pile of texts, reports, and journals when Francine had another breakthrough. "This is it! I think I have found it. Here is a case study that is about the length of the process we are talking about, has good documentation, and has two analyses to share, including one that looks at it from the multiple ethical paradigms and turbulence theory point of view!"

This got Ashley and Sam's attention. Francine held up two articles that described a mentor-protégé relationship at a reforming high school. In this case, the school's first principal served as mentor for her successor. Looking closely at the studies, they did have the ingredients that the Design Team was most interested in. The relationship was long-lived, in this case three years. It was structured carefully with continuous contacts between mentor and protégé and dealt with many of the ethical dilemmas that the Design Team cared so much about. Indeed, in the second article about this example of leadership mentoring, there was a careful analysis of how this pair used multiple ethical lenses to work through ethical dilemmas and how this kind of thinking had a great deal to do with reducing the levels of turbulence that the new principal was feeling.

"I know that we will have to prepare a thoughtful introduction for these articles." Francine saw the need to bring the community along on this one. "Sam, how can we frame the issue in our next report?"

"Well, this does seem to be a good example of many of the ideas that caught everyone's attention earlier in our process. What I'd say in the introduction is this: We want to give the board and community a clear idea of what a leadership mentoring program might look like in some detail. This is important, not only because it shows that it can be done. We also want people to see some of the crucial dynamics and how our concepts of reflective dialogues work when real problems need to be faced. We should tell readers that they are going to see two aspects of the mentoring program. First, they will read about the general qualities of the program and problem-solving dialogues. The second article will highlight the use of multiple ethical paradigms and turbulence theory. I think that this should do. After that, I would simply seek permission to reprint this case study and ask our public to read it."

THE DESIGN TEAM'S CASE STUDY: ARTICLE 1

Passing a Torch:
*Sustaining Change through Leadership Mentoring at One Reforming High School**

Steven Jay Gross
Temple University

ABSTRACT:

While establishing a successful school reform agenda is difficult, sustaining innovation after the departure of the founding leader is even more challenging. This article describes a mentoring program for leadership succession instituted at a reforming high school in the United States. This relationship was officially sponsored by the school district and involved the founding principal (mentor) and her successor (protégé) who agreed to speak daily on the telephone and meet formally for approximately three hours each month over a three-year period. During the 1999–2000 academic year data were collected in the form of interviews and artifacts. Findings showed this relationship concentrated on the school's reform agenda, that a five-stage problem-solving dialogue was used by the mentor and that the new principal was able to work at the encounter, accommodation and educational leadership stages of development. The possible meaning of this model for leadership succession in other school settings is discussed.

INTRODUCTION:

Staying Centered: Curriculum Leadership in a Turbulent Era (Gross 1998) described the combined experiences of ten schools, districts and a teacher-led consortium in the United States and Canada, which had worked for several years in the direction of curriculum, instruction and assessment renewal. Of the qualities that all of the sites shared, effective leadership, usually under the person who initiated the institution's new direction, was an important common attribute. At

---

*Please note that literature reviews for these two articles are incorporated into chapters 2 and 3 of this book and have been cut from this chapter to avoid redundancy. Reprinted with permission from Gross (2002).

the time of that study, only two of the sites had experienced a transition in leadership since starting their new approach. An important question arose: What happens to the agenda of curriculum, instruction, and assessment reform at these sites when a new leader is put into place? A further study, *Life After Moses: The Fate of Selected Innovative Institutions Beyond the Transformational Leader* (Gross 1999), was conducted to begin to answer that question.

One finding of that research showed a range of connection and advice giving between the new leader and the leader who initiated the school's new direction. At one extreme, the new leader had almost no contact with the originating leader. At the other end of the spectrum, there was one case where the new principal and the originating leader entered into a formal mentoring relationship, subsidized by the school district, which is now entering its third year.

1. The purpose of this study is to better understand the dynamics of this mentoring relationship and to document its activities over the course of its first eighteen months.

RESEARCH QUESTIONS:

Specifically, answers to these three questions were sought:

1. Content: To what extent has the mentoring process focused on the school's efforts to sustain its curricular, instructional and assessment renewal?
2. Dynamics of the Mentoring Process: What are the mechanics of the mentor-protégé meetings? Are there patterns?
3. System Implications: Beyond the single school, what might the meaning of this mentoring relationship be in the larger context of this school district or other districts?

METHODOLOGY:

This case study uses qualitative methodology. First, historical perspective was gained through an examination of data (interviews and artifacts) from two previous studies connecting leadership issues and curricular reform at this site. Prior to the start of the interviews, the three of us met to plan the research and consider ways for me to learn about their process without interfering and perhaps to help by asking questions that would aid in their reflections. Eleven interviews with the mentor-protégé pair continued throughout the year. Ten of these were done over the telephone. One was conducted in person. The average length of the interviews was forty minutes. Three of the ten interviews were conducted during a mentoring session and I was able to listen as the pair worked through specific issues of leadership. This was planned so that I would be able to better understand the anatomy of the process that was used in the context of real problems. Several of the interviews were done individually rather than as a pair. I felt that it was important to hear from each alone at times to hear their voice and better understand their priorities as we moved through the academic year. In addition, the superintendent of schools was interviewed to gain his perspective on the mentoring relationship, its impact on the new principal and its possible relevance to other leadership situations in the district. These were augmented with earlier interviews of district administrators and teachers at the school. Finally, early versions of this research were shared with both the mentor and protégé to get their feedback and insights as well as to assure the accuracy of the work.

Artifacts such as the agendas for formal mentoring meetings were analyzed and followed up during subsequent interviews. Using Grounded Theory (Glaser & Straus 1967, Straus & Corbin 1998), these data were recorded, transcribed, coded, sorted, and analyzed in the context of the three key research questions: Content (sustaining curriculum-instruction-assessment renewal), Dynamics of the Mentoring Process (process mechanics), and System Implications (the possible meaning of this model beyond the single school).

Data Sources include: interviews with the mentoring pair over the 1999–2000 academic year; interviews with school personnel, district administrators, students and community members; examination of relevant data from the two previous studies using this school; analysis of documents and other artifacts such as meeting agendas; and e-mail correspondence with the mentoring pair between interviews.

SETTING:

The Rosetta High School (the name used in this study) is set high on a hill and overlooks much of the town of Eastford. While Eastford is a small but growing community, the Rosetta also draws from other communities in the district, including Randolph, a very large community with an urban orientation. At the time of this study, Rosetta had about seven hundred and sixty students in grades nine through twelve. Rosetta had been in the process of innovation since the early 1990's when it completely changed its orientation, joined a national reform group and moved in the direction of shared governance, greater input and responsibility for students in their own learning and strong connection with the communities that it served. The role of shared governance in Rosetta's reform efforts is of particular interest for this research project since many decisions are made in Academic Council, a group comprised of faculty, administrators, parents and students charged with key programmatic decision making. The mentor and protégé spent much time thinking through ways to work effectively with that body. Their seriousness and respect regarding Academic Council were evident throughout the interview sessions as was their awareness of the value of site-based management in comprehensive school reform. How to make these viable as difficult decisions needed to be made became an important element in their deliberations.

Joan Singleton (a name used in this study) was the principal of Rosetta as it moved into its new identity. Her work included guiding the new school in the early years, establishing new norms and procedures as well as representing the school in the community and among her peers and supervisors at the district levels. Joan was highly successful as a principal and Rosetta's first years as an innovative school went well. Rosetta experienced leadership succession when Joan accepted an early retirement. Two years after Joan's departure, Laura Johnston (a name used in this study) became principal. Both Laura and Joan had been successful faculty members at Rosetta before becoming administrators. Both had backgrounds in counseling. As part of her early retirement agreement, Joan needed to perform some service for the district, and, after discussion with Laura and approval of Frank Moorely, superintendent of schools (again a name used in this study), it was decided that the pair would enter into a sustained mentoring relationship.

THE STRUCTURE OF THE MENTORING RELATIONSHIP:

The duration of the relationship was not established in advance, and was subject to review during an annual meeting between Laura, Joan and Frank Moorely. In all, the district supported the mentoring relationship for three years. The data that forms this study comes from the second year of mentoring.

The mentor-protégé relationship that Joan and Laura entered was different from examples found in the literature. [See Table 4.1.] First, it was sustained longer than any of the cases found in previous studies, many of which lasted between a few weeks and a semester. Second, the intensity of the contact also exceeded that of past cases. Joan and Laura spoke on the telephone nearly every night of the school year for about one half hour. They also met for one afternoon each month. The monthly meetings included a written agenda that was faxed to the superintendent's office. Joan also helped by agreeing to facilitate faculty meetings at Rosetta periodically during the school year and in the summer. Finally, Joan and Laura were long-term colleagues and good friends.

It is important to note that this relationship was purely voluntary on all sides. Laura had been a successful vice principal prior to becoming a principal. She was a trusted and valued member of the Rosetta community and nearly everyone acknowledged her ability as a new principal. Likewise, Joan had many other possible ways to serve the district during her early retirement years. She was lionized as a school leader and yet was comfortable moving on after leaving Rosetta.

Table 4.1. Example Mentor–Protégé Relationship

Rosetta	Typical Mentoring/Protégé Program
1. Duration: Three years	Duration: Several weeks to one year
2. Contact: Daily on the phone (30 min) Meetings: Monthly 3–4 hours with additional meetings on weekends as needed	Contact: Varied
3. Connection to the central office $ support from district funds (early retirement package), meeting agendas sent to superintendent's office, formal annual review by all three (mentor, protégé, superintendent)	Connection: Varied, often minimal or connected to higher education institution rather than the district
4. Focus: Sustaining the reform agenda through support of leadership transition.	Focus: Normally, adjustment to the principalship

THE MENTORING RELATIONSHIP DURING THE 1999–2000 SCHOOL YEAR IN LIGHT OF THE RESEARCH QUESTIONS:

1. Content: To What Extent Has the Mentoring Process Focused on the School's Efforts to Sustain Its Curricular, Instructional, and Assessment Renewal?

After reviewing the transcripts of the interviews and examining the artifacts from Rosetta, the connection of the mentoring relationship to the school's innovative efforts in curriculum, instruction and assessment is clear. I will consider that relationship first by highlighting the content of each interview session.

Early Meetings (October–November 1999)

Laura, Joan and I met in August, 1999 to plan the research and series of interviews for the coming school year. At that meeting, Joan and Laura spoke about the year's plans and their workshops with the faculty aimed at trying to help students at Rosetta who were not succeeding academically. Our first interview was held in early October and I was anxious to see how that plan and other plans related to Rosetta's reform efforts were going.

The tone of the first interview was quite serious. Getting the school year off to a good start was complicated by the fact that enrollments were down from earlier projections and there was a risk that faculty jobs might need to be cut. Looming over the school as well were two school evaluations for the academic year: one from the foundation that supported many of Rosetta's reform efforts and the second from the regional accrediting organization. Thus, Joan and Laura needed to work through complex scheduling issues that had serious implications for faculty at the same time as they planned for the school's two evaluations later in the year. While these meetings could be seen as merely administrative, establishing a schedule of classes and confirming faculty job security seem highly relevant to continued reform efforts, as does preparation for two major visitations.

The second set of interviews was conducted separately, one with Laura in late October and the other with Joan in early November. By now, the tone had changed, becoming more optimistic and settled. The early scheduling dilemmas had been worked through and Laura was able to concentrate on issues that were closer to her heart. She spoke about being "more involved with the kids and the teachers," and concentrating less on administrative tasks. Laura was about to return to the key project of the year: helping students with academic difficulties. She and the Academic Council worked on a tutorial program for these students scheduled for four afternoons each week. The first of these sessions was a large success. With Joan's help, the Academic Council became increasingly focused on the instructional program at the school rather than on details. Joan and Laura also helped the group clarify when their meetings and discussions needed to remain confidential. Even with this orientation on instruction and the content of the year's emphasis on helping struggling students, Laura's attention was diverted by the need to plan for a major construction project that was due to start at the end of the school year. Joan added that she helped Laura work through some communication problems with her administrative team as well as Laura's negative reaction when the school did not get technical assistance that it was promised. By winter break, therefore, the mentor and protégé had sustained conversations about issues that related directly to Rosetta's reform goals for the year as well as related administrative issues.

Mid Year Meetings (February–March 2000)

Four interviews took place in February 2000, one with each separately and two when they were together for their monthly problem-solving conference. This was an intense time for Laura. She hurt her back and was in great pain. The school's self-report, so crucial for the accreditation visit, fell on her shoulders as well when the person designated to complete the work was unable to do so. Finally, the construction project started to take important amounts of time as Laura was pulled out of her work at the school to attend meetings at the central office. During these weeks, the content of the interviews shifted from reform efforts to the concrete tasks needed to keep Rosetta running effectively.

The two interviews held during Laura and Joan's monthly meetings focused on the content of Rosetta's reform program. The first of these centered on a personnel issue and how Academic Council could work through this positively and use it to establish policy. In this way, Joan and Laura thought through ways to enhance self-governance at their school. The second meeting dealt with the question of allowing students to take advanced courses. Specifically, the question became one of teacher authority in making these decisions and their role of larger school policy. Again, both mentor and protégé concentrated their energies on ways to get Rosetta's self-governance model to have a central role in working the problem to conclusion. Interestingly, the pair dealt with these questions at the same time as Rosetta's two visitations were held. The foundation visit was something of a disappointment since the review was not outstanding and Laura felt unsupported in her school's efforts. The regional accreditation visit was a different matter. It went quite well and Rosetta was approved for six years without having to hold a midpoint review. Again, the meetings seemed to gravitate toward issues either directly related to Rosetta's reform program or toward enhancing systems, such as self-governance, that were central to the school's reform.

Late Meetings (May–July 2000)

Three interviews were conducted in the spring and early summer 2000. The first was in May and, again, was held during the monthly session between mentor and protégé. The second and third were wrap-up interviews conducted separately with Joan and Laura. While this period spanned the end of the year and the start of summer vacation, the pace of work remained very active. In May, both Joan and Laura were working on the master schedule for the following year. The focus of their discussions was the possible need to cut sections, in one case the possible elimination of a section that was part of an earlier innovation. As will be described in the following section, their work centered on raising the question to the level of principle and the connection of the course to the school's reform mission. Just as in earlier meetings, the pair also dealt with the construction issue and the need to plan for possible disruptions. They also reported that the foundation reevaluated Rosetta, giving the school higher marks for performance.

The July interviews showed that the content of Rosetta's reform agenda was still an integral aspect of the dialogue between Joan and Laura. Both were working with Academic Council to develop plans for a freshman-sophomore house system for the school. This required meeting with a planning team of teachers over the summer to lay the groundwork for such a change and included consultation work as well as facilitation by Joan.

Analysis of the interviews shows a clear and sustained focus on issues directly related to Rosetta's reform program, in the context of the realities of school leadership. School schedules, faculty security, construction plans, and dealing with the loneliness of the job all became subjects for discussion. However, these did not overwhelm the core question of the overall direction of the school, nor the year's emphasis on helping unsuccessful students. By year's end, a support system was in place for these students as well as plans for a freshman-sophomore house system. If anything, the mentor-protégé relationship may have helped Laura to deal with systemic turbulence while it was at a moderate level so that she could maintain a reform agenda (Gross 1998).

2. Dynamics of the Mentoring Process: What Are the Mechanics of the Mentor-Protégé Meetings? Are there Patterns?

Because three of the interview sessions were held during monthly meetings of the mentor and protégé, I was able to listen in as Joan and Laura worked through typical issues together. In all three cases, I was able to ask questions about events at Rosetta and then listen for about forty-five minutes as the pair carefully worked through one of the difficult issues then facing Laura. By transcribing the three sessions and carefully mapping out the stages of dialogue between the pair, I have been able to find interesting patterns in Joan's mentoring style. In brief, Joan carefully guided Laura through five stages of dialogue during each of the three meetings. These included: Stage One—Laying Out the Problem, Stage Two—Working the Issues by Gathering Crucial Information, Stage Three—Placing the Issue in a Larger Context, Stage Four—Preparing to Bring the Issue to the Academic Council, and Stage Five—Understanding the Human Relations Side of the Question. [See Table 4.2.]

Below I will describe the stages that were evident in each of the three meetings.

Table 4.2. Five Stages of Leadership Mentoring Dialogue at Rosetta

1. Laying Out the Problem
   - Chronology of events surrounding the issue
   - Who is involved? Who said what?
   - What underlying dilemma may be involved?
   - What wider implications for the school or district might there be?
2. Working Through the Issue by Gathering Crucial Data
   - What information is missing from stage 1?
   - Where can more points of view be found? (Others to interview)
   - Is there a written record?
3. Analyzing and Organizing Information
   - What does the story from all sources say to us?
   - Are new causes emerging?
   - Is this issue really part of a larger, more complex pattern?
4. Preparing to Bring the Issue to the Shared Governance System (Moving to Action)
   - Action steps taken through shared governance
   - Work cooperatively with shared governance body regarding process.
   - Share data developed in earlier stages.
   - Think through the possible flow of the meeting. Are there possible ways to help facilitate the flow of the next meeting?
5. Understanding the Human Relations Side of the Issue
   - Feelings about key protagonists
   - "What's the worst thing that can happen?"
   - Considering the prevailing mood of the school

Stage One: Laying Out the Problem:

In one session, Joan and Laura worked on a complex personnel problem dealing with funding a part-time position out of a grant. After Laura described the request, Joan started to help her see the complexity of the issue. First, Joan guided Laura through some of the chronology of the grant. Who else was given this part-time position? How did the grant evolve? What was it intended to accomplish? Was there district money involved as well? Next, Joan helped Laura think the request through. What, exactly does this person want? What is this person willing to do? What accountability would there be for this person? Finally, by fleshing out the problem, an ethical dilemma was revealed: If this request is granted, something else in the academic program might have to be cut and that, Laura believed, would not benefit students. Now that most of the problem lay clearly before them, the session took a turn towards the gathering of information.

Stage Two: Working the Issue by Gathering Crucial Information:

Joan made a clear switch in the sessions from trying to understand the problem from Laura's perspective to pointing out the need to gather more information. This allowed the pair to start to work on responding to the problem in a sustained and organized way. In a different session, Joan and Laura were considering the possible elimination of a program. After Laura's description of the issue, Joan pushed for more information. "One thing you have not talked about is hard data." She asked how the teachers of the program spent their time. "You need to have them break down what they do every day so that you have it. Because you don't have any hard data." Now that the issue was raised, Joan helped Laura think about possible sources for information. Where can Laura go for information? Who can she trust to tell her accurate information? She suggested that Laura interview teachers who were currently in the program and to get that information in writing. She also warned Laura to be careful since this is a popular program with some people and there might be a backlash if it were to be challenged. By this point in the meeting, Laura and Joan had agreed on the dimensions of the problem, what facts were currently known and what additional data was needed to engage the issue. Finally, Joan helped Laura devise a thoughtful and sensitive way of gathering more information before taking action.

Stage Three: Placing the Issue in a Larger Context by Organizing Information:

Understanding the dimensions of a problem and working from a well-rounded set of facts is an obvious and important step. However, Joan did not stop there. She consistently emphasized the connection between the current question and related issues. By examining a constellation of relevant problems, she helped Laura to see a wider context and gain perspective. In the March interview the mentor and protégé considered the problem of teachers not allowing students to move from one level of a series of courses to the next. The problem was serious since these series of courses were part of a graduation requirement. After moving through stages one and two, Joan emphasized the larger context of the problem. First, she thought about the issue in terms of the school's reform efforts. "People making decisions without having the global understanding is rearing its head at Rosetta. . . . Site-based management is fine but there is a process." Soon, the conversation moved to another teacher in a different department who was also blocking certain students from taking advanced courses. Joan encouraged Laura through the data-gathering stages and then helped her to think about possible reasons for the problem. What was the history of these students with prior teachers? Were both of these teachers possibly suffering from the high levels of stress in the system that was now so focused on results? What about the person who described the problem to Laura? Was she putting her own emotional spin on things? Finally, Joan suggested an examination of standardized tests results to see approximately how many students were likely affected. By understanding the size of the issue, Laura could more accurately communicate with others who would need to be brought in at the next stage.

Stage Four: Preparing to Bring the Issue to Academic Council:

By this point in the meetings, Joan and Laura had worked through the question and gained some sense of its size, importance and its relevance to other questions at Rosetta. Only after having all of these in place were they ready to work on action steps. In all three cases, Joan helped Laura prepare to take the issue to Academic Council. In this way, Joan kept faith with one key element in Rosetta's reform effort: the creation of site-based management and shared governance. Both Joan and Laura expressed great confidence in their school's model. Joan spoke frequently of the quality and fairness of the people on the council. She also acknowledged that Academic Council needed to return to agreed-upon procedures from time to time. "If people are not following the process, Academic Council needs to revisit that. Site-based management does not mean anarchy."

Thinking through how to share a problem with Academic Council so that it might be dealt with effectively required consideration. In the case of the personnel question described above, Joan suggested that the first step was to ask Academic Council what information they needed to make a decision. Next, she suggested that Laura share the information that she had uncovered on the history of the issue. Third, Joan asked Laura to think of how the meeting might go. Since the teacher involved also sat on the council, was it fair for her to make her request and then participate in the discussion? In the end, they concluded that the council needs to establish the process for making this decision. Laura was now ready to share the problem with Academic Council with the information and ideas for processes that would lead to a reasoned deliberation. Not only had the mentor and protégé thought through the current question, they showed faith in the school's reform structures in a way that they hoped might expand Academic Council's effectiveness.

Stage Five: Understanding the Human Relations Side of the Question:

In all three cases, Joan ended the consideration of the problem by raising human relations issues. With the personnel issue, she asked Laura to describe her greatest fear. "Think about the worst thing that can happen." Laura responded, "She can turn a few people against me." Joan: "Based on what?" Soon, it was clear that Laura's greatest fear was that if this teacher, or any teacher, got [her] way on this issue, it would harm the program for students. Thus, the personal side of the question was changed into a principle that could be dealt with by Academic Council. In the case of the teachers not allowing students to move into the higher-level course, Joan asked Laura to think about general conditions. Joan suggested: "Start a mantra: It is a tired time of the year." The accreditation visit was tough and the staff should be given credit for that. They also reflected that spring break was late this year and Joan asked Laura to get a reading where people were with their work. How many were upbeat?

In the personnel case, Joan ended the session with a careful review of the steps that they worked through together. This might have been because it was complex. It might also have been because it was earlier in the meetings and Laura may have internalized the process well enough by the later meetings to have not needed a direct review of the stages.

CONCLUSION:

These stages were consistent, though in one case stages two and three were reversed. The five stages aimed at lifting the level of discussion from ad hoc problem solving to careful examination of an issue, measured and thoughtful consideration of possible consequences of a variety of different responses and transition of the issue from a principal problem to a question for Rosetta's shared-governance model. By repeating the stages, Joan seemed to have been sharing a habit of mind with Laura. Problems needed to be examined in some detail; often, more information was needed, that information needed to be organized carefully before acting, the assembled information had to be shared with someone or some group, again in an organized fashion, and that group had to be empowered to act in a responsible way.

Understanding how to share information with a decision-making board, whether it was Academic Council, a school board or a board of trustees, is also a learned activity and one that Joan understood well. By asking questions and pointing out possible roadblocks, traps and opportunities, she helped Laura act in an ethical and strategic manner. Thus, the interviews revealed a reasoned, systematic approach to problem solving. The five stages that Joan and Laura observed flowed naturally in their meetings and resulted in a considered plan for action. The dialogues dealt with many aspects of the dilemmas yet did not become stuck in any phase. The mechanics of this extended mentoring model expressed in these five stages give the relationship important structural substance.

QUESTION THREE: BROADER IMPLICATIONS BEYOND THE SCHOOL:

The first two sections of this paper consider the mentorship/protégé process at Rosetta from the perspective of the school alone. If the process did not work effectively in its intended setting, little further comment on the possibilities of this mentoring model beyond the school would make sense. Since the model did connect to important reform content and since it did follow a systematic process that responded to important decision-making roles for the principal, the final research question is appropriate. What implications for extended mentoring of the new principal might there be beyond Rosetta? I will respond to this question in two ways. First, I will consider the meaning of this process from the district perspective based upon an interview with the superintendent. Second, I will examine this mentor-protégé relationship in light of the developmental continuum of new school leaders proposed by Hart and Bredeson (1996).

My interview with the district superintendent was held at the end of the 1999–2000 academic year and revealed his own perspective on the progress of the mentoring relationship. This was important since it was a glimpse into the possible relevance of this mentoring model for schools besides Rosetta. Superintendent Frank Moorely's remarks enhanced my understanding of the model in two ways: first he had a clear sense of some structural reasons for the success of the model and second, he had specific reasons why he felt the model to be effective in the professional development of a new principal in a reforming school.

Moorely pointed out that the mentoring relationship idea may have come from Joan and Laura but that it fit nicely into the district's early retirement plan for administrators. Under the early retirement option, administrators could continue to work for the district for up to five years if they could find a project deemed to be useful. Some projects, like the use of early-retired administrators to help supervise district testing, helped to relieve pressure on building administrators. While Joan and Laura's plan was more focused and long lived, it at least fit into a structure that already existed at the district level. The formal quality of the relationship was also attractive. As was described above, the pair committed to formal agendas of monthly meetings, and an annual review of their work with the superintendent. Moorely was familiar with the content of the meetings and easily mentioned some of the central topics that the pair worked through over the year including the master schedule, grades, and test scores.

The superintendent suggested four qualities about this model that he found attractive. First, the pair started with an established record of trust. "So when they started a formal mentoring, it really just formalized what the reality was already. So you don't have to go through that kind of groundbreaking level of a professional relationship. It was already done. The trust was there, the confidence was there. The belief from both parties that each one was highly competent and valued. . . . And knew what the heck they were doing." According to Moorley, this meant that if there were stages of the mentoring relationship, "it started on the third stage rather than starting down on ground level."

Second, because the mentoring relationship involved the founding leader of Rosetta's reform, the process allowed for stability in the effort to maintain direction. "First of all it has maintained continuity in terms of the leadership style." This continuity was key in helping Rosetta maintain "focus and direction."

The third outstanding quality of this model, from the perspective of the central office, was its direct emphasis on early professional development of new leaders. "It has given that professional support that a new principal needs to have. The ability to have a person that you can have confidential discussions with and not risk a great deal." Later Moorley reflected, "You need to have the chance to be vulnerable. That is what develops principals."

Finally, having an experienced leader mentor a new principal over a sustained period helped the newcomer deal with the complex maze of rules and regulations that are a fact of administrative life. Moorely told me that the Education Code was "two inches thick and fine print. Nobody knows all of that. You have to have a person whom you can ask," to understand. For these important practical matters, Laura could rely on Joan.

Summing up his feelings, Moorely said, "I've watched Laura as a principal grow this past year and the year before that in monumental strides." Clearly, the superintendent showed his support for this model by continuing to support it for three years. He also had specific reasons for his support and showed a good degree of knowledge of both the content and process of the model. Many of his reflections show some support for sustained mentoring of new principals in a larger context.

I will now reflect on this model of mentoring new principals in light of the three-stage developmental continuum described by Hart and Bredeson (1996), which combines essential ideas of current theorists. Hart and Bredeson found that successful principals move from an initial period on the job (Encounter) to a period of adjustment (Accommodation) and arrive at a stage of productive professional work (Stabilization, Educational Leadership and Professional Actualization). Comparing Joan and Laura's mentor-protégé relationship to these stages revealed interesting and potentially useful qualities of the model as it is applied to reforming schools. I will make the argument that Joan helped to guide Laura through all of these phases at the same time, rather than sequentially, as the continuum might suggest.

In the Encounter stage, new principals attempt to survive entry into the leadership role. This includes dealing with strong and entrenched faculty in a positive manner as well as understanding how one fits into the new situation. Stress focused on hurt feelings is common in the Encounter stages. Laura did seem to experience the encounter phase, even though she was a longtime veteran of the school. The reason that she did have to engage with this first stage is that she was new at being the school's leader. This meant redefining herself as someone in charge and accepting Joan's view that being a successful principal meant being alone many times and having to balance many tasks. Especially early in the year Laura experienced the stress of multiple simultaneous demands. "I find myself going in fifty million directions. . . . Will I be talking about construction? Will I be talking to a teacher who's mad at another teacher?"

Many of Laura's other stressful moments were centered on hurt feelings and her sense that she had to be perfect. In mid-winter Laura referred to herself as a type "triple A" personality, always having to be perfect. "I'm my own worst enemy. . . . It's a killer for me." Here again, the nightly discussions and the structured support provided by Joan seem to have helped Laura transfer personal feelings into well-considered administrative behaviors, aligned with Rosetta's reform agenda.

In the Accommodation and Integration stage leaders finish the job of fitting in, connect with the school's culture and experience reduced stress over cyclical activities. Additionally they learn to deal with entrenched resistors to change and distinguish between the group's evaluation and their internal evaluation of their work. It is at this stage that leaders start to accept the ambiguity of their role.

Here Laura's job was one of fitting in as the principal and redefining herself as the school's leader. The second year of mentoring meant that Laura had seen many of the normal facets of the typical school year decisions. Many of these were quite difficult, such as dealing with the possible elimination of classes at the start and end of the year. However, they were surmounted with Joan's help so that the more episodic challenges, such as accreditation, construction, and review by the foundation, could be dealt with effectively.

Many of the events in the interviews were centered on helping Laura confront established powers in a constructive fashion. The personnel issue and the case of the teacher blocking entrance to higher-level courses, discussed above, are two examples. Finally, Laura showed increased willingness to separate the group's evaluation of her work on a given issue from her own view. This was an area of continuing attention, however. In July Joan suggested that Laura needed to see the loneliness of her job and to redefine success. "The sense that you get your satisfaction from the product and that you are not going to get it from people recognizing all of the hard work and hours and saying thank you, that you have to get your strength in other ways."

During the final stage leaders reach Stabilization, Educational Leadership, and Professional Actualization. At this time, the successful leader presses for effective outcomes for the school, rather than for herself. Leaders speak about 'our school.' Thus, decisions are based on what is in the school's best interests, rather than the leader's best interest. At this time, the faculty is empowered to make decisions and work collegially with the principal.

The content of the mentor-protégé meetings connected with all three of these. Laura's concern over accreditation and the foundation review rested much more on the issue of the school's success than on personal gain. The decisions that the pair arrived at, such as which programs to support and which policies to encourage, consistently followed the core beliefs as Laura stated, "The philosophy of the school has always been whatever's best for kids and the closest to the kids is what you keep. That's always been the way and I believe it." Finally, everything that Joan and Laura did in the three monthly sessions described above was designed to find its way to Academic Council, Rosetta's body for faculty empowerment. Many of their decisions were also designed to support the development of that body.

Considering the mentor-protégé model in light of Hart and Bredeson's continuum is quite revealing since it opens up the possibility that mentoring may allow the new principal to develop in all three areas at once, instead of developing in one at a time in a sequential, linear fashion. As was seen above, Laura had a clear connection to all of these stages. This might help to explain Frank Moorely's feeling that Laura improved dramatically during her first two years as principal.

CONCLUSION

This study has revealed early answers to the research questions. The mentor-protégé meetings had a clear and sustained connection to the core content of curriculum-instruction-assessment reform at Rosetta in general and to the theme of supporting the underachieving student in particular. Next the mentor and protégé followed a consistent process during three problem-solving meetings. The five stages that comprise their system were observed, with one exception, in order and in great detail. This demonstrates that there was a clear system in place. Finally, from the perspective of the superintendent, and from Hart and Bredeson's continuum, there are clear connections between the model of mentoring described in this study and the demands of leadership in the larger arena.

One may consider this model to be a unique case that one district stumbled upon. However, after reflecting on the research questions, a different perspective seems plausible. Extended mentoring of the new principal might be an important alternative to the dilemma of finding sustainable effective school leadership. In this model, leaders receive advice as an ongoing part of their work rather than experience a short mentoring relationship followed by a rapid shift into isolation. The relevance of this approach may be even more clear with innovating schools where there is little precedence for many decisions. If long-term mentor-protégé relationships are to occur in a planned way, serious thought might well be given to districts' developing the kind of early retirement service opportunities found in Joan and Laura's school system, thereby opening an officially recognized and rewarded space.

As Joan often said, the principal's job is a lonely one. Ironically, handling that loneliness successfully may require a trusted connection to a mentor for a sustained period of time. This model does provide one possible expression of that kind of extended support for the developing leader in an innovative setting. Instead of seeing this as a weakness, we might more accurately consider the extended mentorship to be a central element in a principal's professional development and a wise use of the expertise found in many of our senior administrators, thus utilizing the principalship as a career with a multi-staged continuum.

Furthering this line of research would likely include pursuing several questions. While the literature does raise the issue of the role of gender in the mentoring relationship, and while Laura and Joan did reflect on the question, a detailed examination of this aspect of mentoring was beyond consideration for the current study. Next, costs of an extended mentoring system like this one, connected to early retirement, need to be examined to see whether or not this model is affordable on a wider scale. Finally, further consideration of the principal's career continuum, including post-service mentoring, referred to in this study need to be further developed to better understand the possibilities of attracting other, extremely talented leaders such as Joan into the service of helping very promising and committed leaders like Laura in the cause of sustaining meaningful school reform.

THE DESIGN TEAM'S CASE STUDY, ARTICLE 2

Using Multiple Ethical Paradigms and Turbulence Theory in Response to Administrative Dilemmas**

Steven Jay Gross & Joan Poliner Shapiro (2004)

RESEARCH QUESTIONS:

In this article we seek to extend our understanding of Gross's (2002) mentor-protégé case by considering the possible relationship of the mentor-protégé partnership in light of Shapiro and Stefkovich's (2001) multiple ethical decision-making paradigms and Gross's (1998) Turbulence Theory. Specifically, we pose these three questions:

1. To what extent has this mentoring case used a process of ethical decision making?

**Reprinted with permission from Gross and Shapiro (2004).

2. How might Turbulence Theory be applied to this case of mentoring?
3. To what extent has ethical decision making and turbulence theory combined in this case, and how might they be related?

METHODOLOGY

This case study uses qualitative methodology. First, historical perspective was gained through an examination of data (interviews and artifacts) from two previous studies connecting leadership issues and curricular reform at this site. Prior to the start of the interviews, one of the authors (Gross), the mentor and protégé met to plan the research and consider ways for me to learn about their process without interfering and, perhaps to help by asking questions that would aid in their reflections. Eleven interviews with the mentor-protégé pair continued throughout the year. Ten of these were done over the telephone. One was conducted in person. The average length of the interviews was forty minutes. Three of the ten interviews were conducted during a mentoring session and Gross was able to listen as the pair worked through specific issues of leadership. This was planned so that he would be able to better understand the anatomy of the process that was used in the context of real problems. Several of the interviews were done individually rather than as a pair. Gross felt that it was important to hear from each alone at times to hear their voice and better understand their priorities as we moved through the academic year. In addition, the superintendent of schools was interviewed to gain his perspective on the mentoring relationship, its impact on the new principal and its possible relevance to other leadership situations in the district. These were augmented with earlier interviews of district administrators and teachers at the school. Finally, early versions of this research were shared with both the mentor and protégé to get their feedback and insights as well as to assure the accuracy of the work.

Artifacts such as the agendas for formal mentoring meetings were analyzed and followed up during subsequent interviews. Using Grounded Theory (Glaser & Straus 1967, Straus & Corbin 1998), these data were recorded, transcribed, coded, sorted, and analyzed in the context of the three key research questions: Content (sustaining curriculum-instruction-assessment renewal), Dynamics of the Mentoring Process (process mechanics), and System Implications (the possible meaning of this model beyond the single school). Finally, the case was reviewed twice again, once through the perspective of Turbulence Theory and then through the lens of the multiple ethical decision-making paradigms. Data Sources include: interviews with the mentoring pair over the 1999–2000 academic year; interviews with school personnel, district administrators, students and community members; examination of relevant data from the two previous studies using this school; analysis of documents and other artifacts such as meeting agendas; and e-mail correspondence with the mentoring pair between interviews. Member checks were conducted in 2001 at the site and again in 2002 during a follow-up interview.

SETTING:

The Rosetta High School (the name used in this study) is set high on a hill and overlooks much of the town of Eastford. While Eastford is a small but growing community, the Rosetta also draws from other communities in the district, including Randolph, a very large community with an urban orientation. Rosetta had about seven hundred and sixty students in grades nine through twelve and was in the process of innovation since the early 1990s. Shared governance, a centerpiece of Rosetta's reform, is of particular interest since the mentor and protégé spent much time thinking through ways to work effectively with Academic Council, a group comprised of faculty, administrators, parents and students.

Joan Singleton (a name used in this study) led Rosetta in its first reform phase. Joan was highly successful as a principal and Rosetta's innovative plan succeeded. Two years after Joan's retirement, Laura Johnston (a name used in this study) became principal. Since Joan needed to perform some service for the district, as part of her early retirement, it was decided that she and Laura would enter into a sustained mentoring relationship. It is important to note that this plan was mutually agreed to by mentor, protégé, and the superintendent of schools.

The district supported the mentoring relationship for three years. The data that forms this study comes from the second year of mentoring. Joan and Laura's relationship was distinguished by these features: First, it was sustained longer than any of the cases found in previous studies. Second, they worked in a highly structured and carefully focused manner. Joan and Laura spoke on the telephone nearly every night of the school year for about one half hour. Their monthly four-hour meetings included a written agenda that was faxed to the superintendent's office.

MENTORING—USING MULTIPLE ETHICAL PARADIGMS AND TURBULENCE THEORY AT ROSETTA

Learning to become an effective principal in a reforming school certainly includes understanding rapidly shifting conditions. For the mentor and the protégé in this case, understanding and responding effectively to volatile issues and environment was of particular importance. Because of its central focus on analyzing fast-paced change, Turbulence Theory was selected as one lens through which to investigate the dynamics of this mentoring relationship.

Turbulence was a part of the protégé's working life throughout the mentoring relationship. It would be useful to think of the turbulence surrounding the school's leader in the spheres where it most clearly occurred. [Figure 4.1] depicts just such a series of locations including personal-, faculty-, district- and foundation-related issues. [Figure 4.2] places those same issues into the context of the mentoring relationship. Taken together, we can appreciate the different places where turbulence was easiest to detect as well as the valuable overview of the combined turbulence issues seen by the mentor.

Below, we discuss turbulence in each category starting with a turbulence gauge. The purpose of the gauge is to help describe the level of turbulence in each category: personal, faculty, district, and foundation. Accordingly, each turbulence gauge is constructed as a rubric, each uses the common degrees of turbulence (light, moderate, severe, and extreme). Each gauge also includes a description of turbulence at each level as it is applied to the category. For instance, there is a specific description of light, moderate, severe, and extreme turbulence as it applies to the principal's personal issues. By reviewing turbulence in each of the categories with the turbulence gauge we will be better able to speak specifically to degrees of disturbance and the work of the mentoring relationship to bring things better under control.

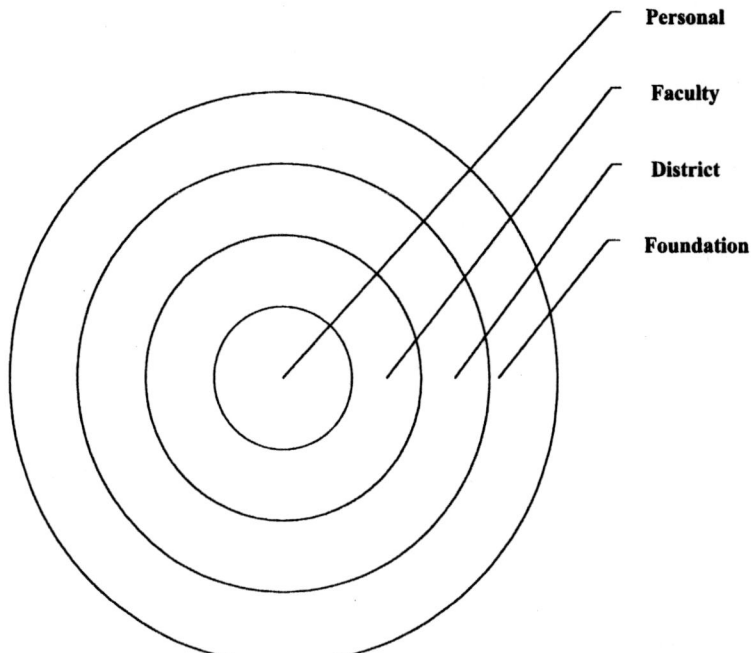

Figure 4.1. Areas of Turbulence Dealt with During the Mentor-Protégé Dialogues

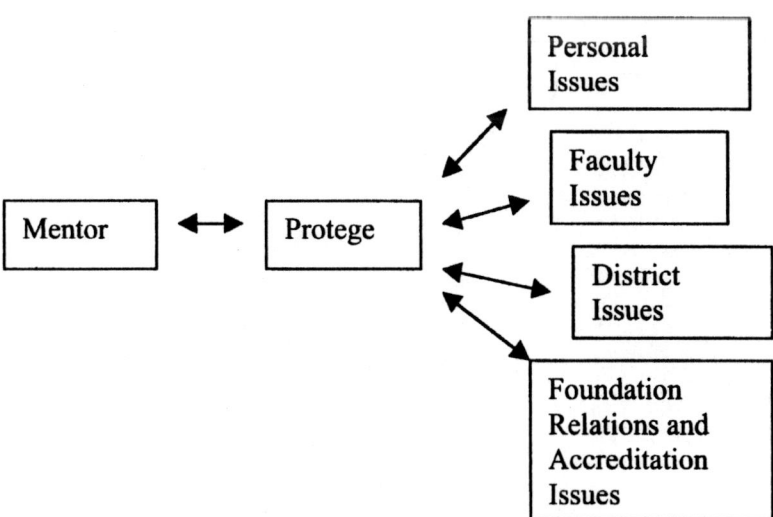

Figure 4.2. Mentor–Protégé Relationship as it Operated on Turbulence Areas

Principal's Personal Issues:

[Table 4.3] illustrates a turbulence gauge for the dimension of the principal's personal issues. While the protégé was successful in the transition into leadership, physical stress and emotional disappointment at the severe level were evident. Much attention was directed at these issues so that an overall moderate level of turbulence could be maintained throughout the mentoring relationship. In one instance, the protégé was disappointed that the faculty took her hospitality for granted when they did not thank her for bringing refreshments to a meeting. The mentor helped her to see the incident in a larger perspective, thereby reducing the hurt of the situation. The mentor also helped her protégé understand the line that is crossed when one becomes the principal. The protégé continued to work on her approach to the principal's job by thinking through her need to drive herself. Calling herself a triple type A personality, she said, "I'm my own worst enemy. It's a killer for me." Her mentor worked closely on this aspect of professional growth by emphasizing the need to detach one-

Table 4.3. Turbulence Gauge for Principal's Personal Issues

Degree of Turbulence	Turbulence as It Is Applied in This Situation
Light: Associated with ongoing issues, little or no disruption in normal work environment, subtle signs of stress	Smooth transition. New principal easily grasps new role. Collegial relationships abound. Visionary leadership. Physical/emotional tranquility for principal.
Moderate: Widespread awareness of the issues, specific origins.	Measured progress in transition with support. New role opens up in the first few months. Principal sees self as a leader and a bit ahead of the school. Physical/emotional stress exists but can be handled with help.
Severe: Fear for the entire enterprise, possibility of large-scale community demonstrations, a feeling of crisis.	Transition blocked. Now growing role confusion. Constantly questions self as leader. Physical/emotional stress getting the upper hand.
Extreme: Structural damage to the reform movement is occurring; collapse of the reform seems likely	Transition a constant losing battle. Confusion of role, vacillating from overcontrol to undercontrol without a center. Plans to leave principal's job as soon as possible. Physical/emotional stress careening out of control. Health at risk.

self from the situation from time to time and to strive for a more systematic problem-solving strategy. The struggle to move beyond personal difficulties continued but at a lower level of turbulence. The mentor's use of the ethic of care to help the protégé endure disappointments and hurt can be seen throughout this case. The mentor worked through the difficulties and helped the protégé rise above pettiness. She moved the principal towards the ethic of the profession and away from the personal in her phone calls and face-to-face meetings. This constant presence of sanity and professionalism had to be helpful to the principal. Additionally, the mentor was able to use the ethic of critique, when appropriate, to assist the principal in distancing herself to notice when she was using her "triple type A personality."

Faculty-Administration Issues:

There were numerous issues surrounding the Rosetta faculty that became the topic of discussion for the mentor and protégé. Before the year even started, the school faculty and administration came together at a retreat and planned for the year's academic focus. The feeling among this group was that students who were failing needed strong attention with specific interventions designed to improve their school experiences. This theme became essential for the year, with the school's shared-governance model, the Academic Council, taking responsibility. The mentor and protégé spent a good deal of time keeping these efforts on track, with good results. Early in the year, an enrollment dip caused great concern for the protégé since that might have resulted in closing sections and cutting faculty positions. Finally, the school's Academic Council was challenged with small but important issues, including handling one teacher's request for funding a part-time position out of a grant, the possible elimination of a popular program, and the case of teachers not allowing students to take advanced courses. Each of these could have escalated into a severely turbulent condition. Through the mentoring relationship, the protégé was able to consider each issue in detail and map out responsive strategies (Gross 2002).

In the area of faculty-administration relations, although not explicitly stated, in analyzing the mentoring relationship, the multiple ethical paradigms were indeed utilized. For example, the shared governance model presented challenges for both the mentor and protégé that required ethical decision making. In shared governance, a great deal of time was spent on professional ethics—or keeping the academic efforts on track, on the part of the mentor. During difficult times, such as the enrollment dip that led to the closing of sections and cutting of faculty positions, the mentor had to focus, not on the ethic of the profession, but on the ethic of care. The protégé needed to be supported in carrying out difficult professional tasks. At this time, the ethic of critique had to also be introduced. The protégé needed the mentor to ask the difficult questions related to the cutting of faculty to remind the protégé why such drastic actions had to be carried out. Additionally, the ethic of justice had to be taken into consideration in not allowing students to take advanced courses. The lack of advanced courses might lead to parents turning to the courts for assistance feeling that their children's needs were not met. Overall, the ethic of the profession was maintained in faculty-administration relations primarily through the mentor who constantly reminded her protégé to put student learning at the center in all of her decisions.

In the area of faculty-administration relations, the evidence pushes in the direction of moderate turbulence [Table 4.4]. The early issue of enrollment could have caused enough dismay to move the faculty to severe turbulence vis à vis the administration. However, the decision was made not to give faculty too much information for fear that this could cause more stress and turbulence for the principal and faculty. Thus, the mentoring relationship led to a decision to contain the turbulence of the enrollment issue to the principal's office.

District Issues:

Interviews with district leaders showed that there was support for Rosetta's reform efforts, at least in name. This was a complex district with many students attending numerous high schools. While Rosetta's work was of serious interest, there were numerous priorities elsewhere. This being said, it is important to point out that the mentoring relationship itself had district approval and was funded by district resources. The superintendent was not only informed of the mentoring meetings, an agenda for each monthly meeting was faxed to his office

Table 4.4. Turbulence Gauge for Faculty/Administration Issues

Degree of Turbulence	Turbulence as It Is Applied in This Situation
Light: Associated with ongoing issues, little or no disruption in normal work environment, subtle signs of stress	Strong support all around. Academic Council working without a problem. Everyone views reform priorities in a similar manner.
Moderate: Widespread awareness of the issues, specific origins	Support evident, personnel issues do arise. Academic Council needs help to work well. Agreement on year's targets. Help needed to stay focused.
Severe: Fear for the entire enterprise, possibility of large-scale community demonstrations, a feeling of crisis	Fractured faculty, dissent growing. Academic Council hostile to year's reform target. Faculty alienated from administration and from Academic Council. No agreement to continue reform efforts.
Extreme: Structural damage to the reform movement is occurring; collapse of the reform seems likely	Faculty alienated from administration and from Academic Council. No agreement to continue reform efforts.

and the mentor-protégé team met with the superintendent annually to review progress and evaluate possible continuation of the relationship.

On the other side, there were important distracters for the principal that seemed to originate at the district level. First, there was a sense that Rosetta was isolated in its reform efforts. Leaders at other district schools were sympathetic but were not engaged in emulating Rosetta's chosen direction and there were times when the protégé felt that she had no clearly supportive peers in the district. Conversations with the mentor appeared to be helpful in this regard by giving the protégé a sense of perspective. Further, district plans for construction became burdensome for the protégé. Quickly scheduled meetings away from the Rosetta campus to work with architects took time away from pressing concerns. Ongoing policies such as the start of the year enrollment problem became a near crisis since Rosetta's drop in students threatened to eliminate class sections and teaching positions.

The use of multiple ethical paradigms was highly relevant, especially in helping the protégé work with the district. The district's initial approval and follow-through on this mentoring relationship showed an ethic of care and an ethic of the profession on the part of the superintendent. Here was a district where school reform counted. On the other hand, Rosetta was the only school with this type of reform agenda. It was essential that the mentor speak with the protégé to make certain that the new leader did not feel isolated. The ethics of care as well as critique were invaluable in this situation as there was a need to make certain that the protégé was supported in this reform and it was also important that the protégé realized that her school was different from the rest. She needed to be able to critically analyze her position in the district, understand what was expected of her and her students, and realize how unique these expectations were in her district.

District-principal issues were characterized by moderate turbulence [Table 4.5]. The enrollment issue and the construction project were clear distracters and increased sense of turbulence. Frequent communications between the principal (protégé), mentor and superintendent throughout the mentoring process seemed related to better understanding of the school's unique needs and potential for the district's overall goals of reform.

Table 4.5. Turbulence Gauge for District Issues

Degree of Turbulence	Turbulence as It Is Applied in This Situation
Light: Associated with ongoing issues, little or no disruption in normal work environment, subtle signs of stress	Coordinated effort supporting reform. Fully supportive of needed work in word and in action. School protected from outside distracters.
Moderate: Widespread awareness of the issue, specific origins.	Understanding of reform and generally sympathetic feelings from the top. Supportive in word, not always in action. Reform not always protected from outside distracters.
Severe: Fear for the entire enterprise, possibility of large-scale community demonstrations, a feeling of crisis.	Unaware of reform priorities. No coordination attempted. Unsympathetic to school generally. Serious outside distracters common.
Extreme: Structural damage to the reform movement is occurring. Collapse of the reform seems likely.	Opposed to core reform agenda. Conflicting priorities abound, resulting in constant derailing distracters.

Foundation and Accreditation Issues:

During the year in question, Rosetta was scheduled for site visits both from an important foundation and from a regional accreditation organization. Both of these were high-profile projects that focused on Rosetta's reform program and promised to draw attention to the school's leadership as well as its faculty, students and staff. Foundation support was deemed essential for the continuation of reform and accreditation was equally a cornerstone. Moderate turbulence was evident for these two issues from the protégé's perspective since it was impossible to ignore either issue and since neither one was a normal part of the school's life [Table 4.6]. At first, it seemed as though normal administrative processes would pull the school through. However, there was a drift into severe turbulence when it became clear that the bulk of the self-reports would fall to the principal. The protégé raised the problems associated with these visitations in conversations with the mentor and was given a forum to think through the problems and choices. Frustration and isolation were replaced with methodical dialogue and coaching and conditions calmed down to the moderate level. Both visits were successful.

Table 4.6. Turbulence Gauge for Foundation and Accreditation Issues

Degree of Turbulence	Turbulence as It Is Applied in This Situation
Light: Associated with ongoing issues, little or no disruption in normal work environment, subtle signs of stress.	Green light. Continued funding assured. New projects called for as current initiatives are deemed successful. Excellent communications. School is considered a model for foundation's current priorities.
Moderate: Widespread awareness of the issues, specific origins.	Visits are ongoing. Satisfactory progress on current projects. Strong communications.
Severe: Fear for the entire enterprise, possibility of large-scale community demonstrations, a feeling of crisis.	Visits and evaluations are not successful. Threat of diminished funding. Priorities are not mutual. Communications obstacles exist.
Extreme: Structural damage to the reform movement is occurring; collapse of the reform seems likely.	End of funding and end of the relationship.

The multiple ethical paradigms were of value in keeping the protégé calm during a difficult and challenging time when a great deal fell on her shoulders. But she was not alone. The mentor, employing the ethic of care, was there to support her. Additionally, at this time, the ethic of the profession was used by the mentor to keep the protégé on track.

The overall estimate is that mentoring was related to sustaining or moving the protégé to moderate turbulence. This is a worthy goal for two reasons: first, a reforming high school with a new leader might not be a likely place for light turbulence at all. That may be too optimistic. Second, moderate turbulence is not necessarily a negative force. The energy from the dynamic conditions may be constructive, opening new possibilities since the status quo is not comfortable. Moderate turbulence has an embedded agenda for further action.

CONCLUSION

Realizing what the level of turbulence is in a dilemma can make a difference in allowing those who are part of the dilemma to step outside the situation and observe it from a distance. The same holds true for analyzing the various ethics. Knowing which ethics a person favors when making a decision tells the individual something about him- or herself and how to deal with the problems. Both concepts offer educators new understandings, insights and options.

In this particular illustration, the mentor gave the protégé constant assistance. This help used multiple ethical frames. All of the four frames were used to solve each of the major problems in this case. However, three of the four ethics were utilized the most in this case. The ethic of justice appeared to be drawn upon less frequently by the mentor with the protégé, but it was used when appropriate. In this case, then, the utilization of the three ethics of care, critique and the profession began to bring the turbulence level down.

A good example of this had to do with the upcoming site visits from an important foundation and from a regional accreditation organization. At the beginning of the year, the principal was very worried about these visits. However, using the ethics of care and critique, over time, the mentor guided the principal and calmed the situation down. This calming of the situation lowered the turbulence level. Thus, in dealing with the problems related to the site visits, the utilization of the multiple ethical lenses worked well with turbulence theory.

Overall, it is our belief that turbulence theory and the multiple ethical perspectives can provide educational leaders with new and rational ways to solve difficult problems. In this case, the mentor and protégé's relationship was enhanced through the use of three ethics—care, critique and the profession. Because the mentor drew upon the different ethics, the protégé was helped both intellectually as well as emotionally. It is interesting to note that the mentor was not trained in the diverse forms of ethics. In this instance, because the mentor worked with the protégé in the past and genuinely wished to help her, intuitively she used the ethics of care and critique. In addition, because the mentor had been an outstanding professional herself, she felt it to be her moral obligation to assist her protégé in the ethic of the profession and sometimes in the ethic of justice. Further, the mentor wanted to make the protégé more comfortable and able to act. To accomplish this, it was necessary to lower the level of turbulence. And this is what she succeeded in doing by using appropriate ethics and by giving excellent advice. Of course, it was important that trust was part of this relationship so that the protégé welcomed the mentor's advice and followed it.

Our hope is that future mentors will have the knowledge base and understandings to assist their protégés in responding to ethical dilemmas. This can happen if educational administration programs offer preparation in ethical decision making, providing multiple paradigms, and it can occur if educational administration programs teach their students turbulence theory. We hope that educational leaders will have these kinds of preparation and opportunities in the future.

CONCLUSION

Ashley, Sam, and Francine presented their selection of articles to the group and waited for a reaction.

"The point was, I suppose, to show us and then the board what a program in the spirit of ours really looks like, is that it?" asked Betty.

"Right. You see, we found it easy to pick out the literature, and it was not that hard to find a strong theory on which to hang all of this." Sam Grey was becoming more comfortable with the flow of the report from his team. "But we have got to remember the people who are going to be asked to pay for all of this but who are not educators. That is why we wanted a clear example."

Francine jumped in. "Betty, we know that almost no one in the community is an expert in this. We also know that up to 80% of all taxpayers do not have children in our schools. That means we have a communications job ahead of us."

Superintendent Betty Clark and the district board chair smiled at each other. "Now you're sounding like thoughtful district leaders trying to develop a base of support. It looks as though this committee has led to a great deal of learning above and beyond the content of leadership mentoring. But what can you tell the public about the combined lessons of both articles? Why was it important to include them both?"

Sam and Ashley had dealt with this question when Francine first proposed the articles. Ashley decided to sum up their reasons.

"Look, Betty, we want to conclude our presentation to the board by answering that one. Here is what we think at this point.

"The power of the first article is that it gives us a flavor of mentoring during a sustained period of time. The fact that this pair worked together for three years, supported by their district, makes a strong statement about commitment on everyone's part.

"Besides commitment, the article spells out many of the technical details of mentoring that we may want to borrow, such as frequency of meetings, use of agendas, and the role of the superintendent.

"Third, the method used by the mentor to probe issues was systematic and, we believe, highly effective. Because it was emphasized regularly, it amounts to a problem-solving strategy through dialogue. We believe that this can be taught to prospective mentors as well in our own program.

"As much as we learned from the first article, we were still left with the question of where the central theory belonged. After all, if we are so convinced of the use of multiple ethical paradigms and turbulence theory, where can we show that to the board? If this case study is so useful, where will we find the theory we care about? The answer is that this case study was a clear example of multiple ethical paradigms and turbulence theory working together. The mentor and protégé not only had a systematic way of problem solving, as we saw in the first article; they also had a rich, strategic process that used these theories. This makes the second article a crucial addition because it shows theory in practice, and it shows just how practical they are in helping a protégé respond to the pressures of the principal's job."

"Well, that is pretty convincing to me," Antonio Bruski was serious. "At first, I was wondering just like Betty. Now, I think you've got a logical set of conclusions. What I'd ask you to do is add these points into the written record and be prepared to explain them in person as well."

Francine, who started this phase of the Design Team's work with her offer to leave the group, ended this session with a different kind of alarm. "Antonio, that's a good idea, but our case studies raise another problem. Just think about it. We do have a real-life example that shows our ideas in action, I will grant you. But does anyone really think that every mentor and every protégé will automatically operate in this way? I mean, how are we going to make sure that the mentors and protégés are this successful? After the presentation of this part of our work is done, and if the board accepts it, our next task is building a model, right? Well, that's got to be the place where we have to make it clear that our specific approach to leadership mentoring will be consistent. We need to have a content, a way of learning, and a way of showing progress. This has to be the place where we are clear about the skills for both mentor and protégé. We may not be able to count on mentors all having the natural gifts of the woman in our case studies, but we can make darn sure that everyone who wishes to become a mentor in Randolph learns them."

CHAPTER 5

The Design Team Builds a Model of Leadership Mentoring

The Design Team's presentation of the two articles was well received. As one community member remarked, "Okay! First, I appreciate the specifics. These women are evidence that what you're talking about is possible. Don't get me wrong, I believed you, but it was getting just a little too ivory tower for me. Sam, no offense, but you sold me when you acknowledged that we're not all university faculty members!" This caused the speaker, Sam, and most of those in attendance to laugh.

Another person in the audience helped conclude the evening by referring to the next step. "All right. I see how you've taken your time building up to this stage. You're ready, and we're ready to see a plan. This is where we'll want some detail and some sense of how you intend to make your ideas operational." At its regular meeting, the Design Team got an immediate assist from Ronnie. "There is one thing I am sure about when I think of our situation. We are at the point where either our ideas come together or the whole enterprise falls apart. So, I have been reflecting a lot. We may want to take a page out of the curriculum projects that the district has been creating for the past several years. They follow a similar set of steps and cover most issues, and they have the advantage of being familiar to the board, faculty, administration, and even the community. What we need to do is to organize all of the work we've done so far into three elements: Curriculum, Instruction, and Assessment."

Ashley and Warren were experienced in this process as well and seemed nearly convinced. "Look, Ronnie, I think that the basic idea is sound, and I can imagine it working out for us," Warren knitted his brow as he spoke. "But I am not really comfortable with those exact words. I mean, we're describing a partnership here. Those words sound like the classroom and may come across as a bit heavy-handed." That is why the group decided to do a little adjusting. "Curriculum" became "Content," "Instruction" became "Interactive Learning," and "Assessment" became "Attainment." At this point, Zbigniew smiled wryly and said with more than his normal irony, "This is now dignified and appropriate language. Do you think that we'll be able to treat kids with this much respect some day?" The district staff felt the same way. If this was good enough for two adults, maybe ideas such as interactive learning and attainment made sense for young people as well.

Having agreed to an organizing set of ideas, it was now possible to review all of the previous reports and code them. Materials were marked either content, interactive learning (that is, how the content might be effectively shared), or attainment (or how protégé and mentor could demonstrate continuous learning of the content). Because the task was so clearly divided, pairs of Design Team members could work on the elements together, thereby speeding up the task of creating the model. After all of the information was coded, it was placed in a logical order resulting in the emerging model of leadership mentoring.

THE DESIGN TEAM'S MODEL FOR LEADERSHIP MENTORING IN THE RANDOLPH SCHOOL DISTRICT

Perspective

The Leadership Mentoring Model is *not* a one-way street. It is not the case that a person is simply a mentor or a protégé. It is important for the protégé to see that she or he is also responsible to be generative. For instance, a school leader needs to help new teachers, staff members, and people new to beginning administrative positions. The model is designed to help the protégé to become a mentor in turn to these people. We aspire to create a community that is nurturing, generative, and designed to grow at the individual and group levels.

Foundational Values of the Leadership Mentoring Model

The Leadership Mentoring Model embraces the concept of responsibility over mere accountability. This means that both mentor and protégé work from an internal motivation rather than one that is imposed from above. It is also one that uses the emerging ideas in the field of educational leadership. One example of this new perspective is the New DEEL movement now taking hold in departments of educational leadership and policy studies in North America and Australia. The "DEEL" in New DEEL stands for Democratic-Ethical Educational Leadership. The New DEEL's mission statement describes a dynamic kind of school leader who is versed in ethical decision making, educational leadership, and community engagement locally and beyond:

> The mission of the New DEEL is to create an action-oriented partnership, dedicated to inquiry into the nature and practice of democratic, ethical educational leadership through sustained processes of open dialogue, right to voice, community inclusion, and responsible participation toward the public common good. Further, the New DEEL seeks to create an environment to facilitate democratic ethical decision-making in educational theory and practice which acts in the best interest of all students. (Gross & Shapiro, 2005, p. 1)

This means that there are certain values for leadership mentoring and its curriculum. Chief among these is the conscious emphasis on differentiating this kind of leadership training from that found in corporations. Clearly, there are good management practices that can be transferred from businesses to schools. However, there is a fundamental difference between the two, and that has to do with responsibility. In a corporation, the primary fiduciary responsibility of management is to stockholders. This is not an opinion but a well-accepted legal requirement. Schools, on the other hand, have direct responsibility to students, their families, and their communities. In the United States, public schools operate under the control of the state, but they serve young people. Thus, the metaphor often held as an example for educators to follow of the school as a well-managed corporation falls apart rather quickly. This is not surprising if we consider the advice of Gareth Morgan (1997), who wrote that all metaphors both illuminate and obscure. The illuminating quality of the school-as-business metaphor does exist, but what is obscured is the fact that principals are not CEOs. Their ethical and moral responsibilities carry them into the community, into the field beyond their district, and, at times, into courts to pursue what is best for their students. That is why the ideas of such groups as the New DEEL represent a potential philosophical foundation for the emerging new school leader. These values are also built into this model of leadership mentoring by the content of ethical decision making and the direction of related readings. Since the Design Team believes that there is no value-neutral leadership, we have worked to establish a consistent direction for leadership development in our district and hope that this will help us to attract and nurture leaders who share that vision. We further acknowledge that this kind of leadership is expected from mentors, and we expect mentors to be models of these dynamic principles. By centering much of our leadership mentoring program on multiple ethical paradigms and turbulence theory and emphasizing specific content, the Design Team seeks to respond to concerns that mentoring will only result in passing along bad habits from one generation of school leader to the next by merely socializing the new principal (Crow & Matthews 1998). While we believe that this pathology/contagion metaphor is overblown, we do recognize the potential risk and believe that our model represents a thoughtful response.

THREE INTEGRATED FOCI: CONTENT, INTERACTIVE LEARNING, AND ATTAINMENT

The model for leadership mentoring is broken into three main areas. These are content, interactive learning, and attainment. In practice, these three act very much like the curriculum, instruction, and assessment triangle that we see in typical programmatic design (see Gross

1998 for example). The terms have been altered slightly so that they fit more comfortably with the mentor-protégé relationship, which is one of adult-to-adult learning. It is vital to see these three areas as dynamically related. If we say that content is the learning agenda and call that C, and interactive learning is the way we share the learning agenda and call that I, and attainment is how we determine progress on the learning agenda and call that A, we have a triangle— a CIA triangle. But this is a *dynamic* triangle, or what may be called a "rubber-band triangle." In the case of the leadership mentoring model, the content is focused on the developing needs of the protégé. Here, there is content that centers upon the conditions of the principal's job, on ways to respond effectively to the job, and on gaining perspective on the mentor-protégé relationship in resolving various levels of problems. By its nature, this kind of content lends itself to interactive learning (the I in the CIA triangle). This is not the time for lectures or too much isolated reading and writing. It is a time for dialogue and reflection. Attainment, the third element in the triangle, is also interactive. How could we construct a standardized test for this kind of mentoring program when so much of its value is gained in the intense interaction between the mentor-protégé team? Yet, without the attainment (the A in our triangle), we would not be able to demonstrate progress in learning to apply the content. In this way, we have a systematic approach to organizing the program. Each aspect is designed to mesh with the other two. Each is designed to coordinate easily. While each site will add detail, making this program a more exact fit to local conditions, the general principles described in this section will place each mentor-protégé pair on an effective path. It would help not to think of this model as an exact building plan for a specific kind of home. That would be a one-size-fits-all approach and not sensitive to local differences. Instead, this model is more like a building code. If you follow it, no matter what the specifics of any given school may be, you can have confidence that the program will operate well and that you have not ignored important elements. Your building will very likely stand.

CONTENT: THE C IN CIA (THE LEARNING AGENDA)

1. *Understanding the difficulties facing today's principals.* It is crucial for the protégé and mentor to have a common understanding of the state of the principalship today. This will help both to place the specifics of events in the school in a wider context and help the protégé to see her or his challenges more objectively. Three kinds of reading are strongly advised:

- Generational shifts and other demographic changes in school leadership patterns.
- Specific pressures embodied in the role of principal.
- The history of educational movements over the past century with special attention to their impact upon school leadership. These should include philosophical as well as applied perspectives and cover the core arenas of curriculum, instruction, and assessment.

2. *Mentoring as a response to the difficulties of being a new principal.* This may seem obvious. However, in the throes of busy times, it will help to see that mentoring is a well-respected response to the needs of new school leaders. Understanding the wider community of mentors and protégés may also give the pair needed information on ways to improve their own work and an opportunity to network nationally and internationally. Three kinds of readings are of particular note in this dimension:

- Examples of mentoring at the district, state, regional, national, and international levels
- Key qualities of successful programs
- Limitations to mentoring and caveats

3. *Qualities of a good mentor.* While this may seem self-evident, the literature shows just the opposite. Work such as Mertz's (2004) opens up a range of possible relationships that may be helpful but are

not, according to her, true mentoring. This kind of reading can lead to sustained discussions and some constructive introspection for both parties. Just as important, this kind of reading can lead to common understandings of expectations for the mentor.

4. *Qualities of a good protégé.* Similar to understanding the role of the mentor, it is crucial that depictions of a good protégé are included. Like all human activity, this is a dynamic and evolving role. The protégé is in a period of striking growth and development, not static passive need. Both parties need to recognize the responsibilities of the protégé. The literature cannot be expected to provide ironclad rules for protégé or mentor. It offers something far more useful: an intelligent range of ideas that should lead to serious discussion.

5. *Overview of key ideas for mentors to share with protégés.* Especially during the first year of the principalship, the ideas in this section will be crucial elements of the new leader's day and will be the center of many discussions. If the mentor comes from the same district as the protégé, there will likely be familiarity with district-specific practices. Mentors coming from beyond the district need to learn local expectations as part of their orientation into mentoring. One way of considering these topics is to reflect on Maslow's (1970) hierarchy of needs. Many of the issues below would fit into the basic needs that are described in that construct and are probably fundamental to the more creative possibilities of building leadership. Later content topics will help the protégé move to a broader understanding of school leadership. The transition from building manager to educational leader is critical and one that many principals never make. By sequencing readings, discussions, and other leadership mentoring activities carefully, the program is designed to increase the likelihood of that kind of growth.

- Concrete technical aspects of the job
  - Daily operations
  - Information collection, problem-solving strategies for these tasks

- Ways to work with a variety of adults
- Time management in the face of multiple tasks (Cordeiro & Smith-Sloan 1995)
- Becoming more broadly effective
  - Mapping the school's politics
  - Empowering people
  - Aligning the structure to the job at hand
  - Celebrating the school's culture
  - Reframing using a variety of perspectives to understand a problem
- Understanding the protégé's likely stages of development
  - Initial contact
  - Liminal stage
  - Settling-in stage
  - Efficacy stage
  - Interdependence stage (Cordeiro & Smith-Sloan 1995)
- Multiple ethical paradigms and turbulence theory: the keys to dealing with ethical dilemmas (Gross & Shapiro, 2004)
  - The ethics of justice, care, critique, and the profession
  - The four levels of turbulence and the construction of the turbulence gauge
  - The dialogue blending MEP/TT
  - Consider the turbulence level
  - Consider the four ethical lenses
  - Decide upon a course of action emphasizing one or more of the ethical lenses
  - Estimate the change in turbulence that may result from the course of action
  - Understanding these in the context of the hypothetical case as written by the Design Team
- Leadership mentoring in real time (Gross 2002; Gross & Shapiro 2004)
  - Comparing and contrasting the case study to that of each mentor-protégé pair
  - Dynamics of the mentor-protégé process and the five-step dialogue

- Laying out the problem
- Working the issue by gathering crucial information
- Placing the issue in a larger context by organizing information
- Preparing to bring the issue to a shared-governance meeting
- Understanding the human relations side of the question
- Understanding the case study in the context of multiple ethical paradigms and turbulence theory

INTERACTIVE LEARNING FOR THE LEADERSHIP MENTORING MODEL PROGRAM

Shared Readings

Several of the reports of the Design Team include references to important findings in the literature on leadership mentoring as described in the content section of this model. These should be read by the mentor and the protégé and used as examples to draw from, especially in the early days. The shared readings must also include a collection of documents from the school, district, state, and national levels, *blended into the schedule of meetings as they relate to the development of the protégé.* The Design Team believes that care should be taken not to overwhelm the protégé with so many rules and regulations at first that she or he is not able to reflect creatively. The selection of key documents and how they are shared will have a great deal to do with the success of the program.

In addition, the mentor should be strongly encouraged to deepen his or her understanding of the literature on mentoring by continuing to read the emerging literature on mentoring and by sharing new insights with the protégé. The purpose of the common readings from the literature review and case study is to create a shared perspective on the content and process of leadership mentoring. This will help to facilitate dialogue between the mentor and protégé and act as a lens with which to consider new ideas and points of view.

Interactive Meetings

Taking direction from Crocker and Harris (2002), the Design Team believes that mentors should remember the four-step-strategy approach and plan their work accordingly. These steps include:

- Teaching the protégé how
- Letting her or him do
- Helping her or him learn from having done
- Accepting her or him unconditionally

Even in the first stage of teaching the protégé how to do a task or how to think a problem through, we believe that the mentor should take a collaborative, hands-on approach rather than a didactic, lecturing one. During the early phases especially it is crucial for the mentor to remember the developmental stages that many new leaders go through described above (initial contact, liminal phase, settling in, efficacy, and interdependence). Understanding these stages and creating learning experiences that meet the protégé where she or he is along that continuum will go a long way toward making sure that communication is positive, appropriate, and effective.

Integrating Two Essential Mentoring Dialogues

There are two kinds of dialogues that need to take place in the leadership mentoring meetings.

1. Using the Five-Step Problem-Solving Process

First, mentors need to make consistent use of the problem-solving dialogue described in the case study:

- Laying out the problem
- Working the issue by gathering crucial information
- Placing the issue in a larger context by organizing information

- Preparing to bring the issue to a shared governance meeting
- Understanding the human relations side of the question

Practice in this approach for mentor and protégé is intended to create a habit of mind or disposition for the pair as they face the inevitable flow of new challenges that are part of any principal's life. Looked at one way, this could seem confining since there are five discrete steps in the discussion and they need to be followed in order. Looked upon in a different way, following this process is similar to honoring a well-respected meditation. At first, it may feel a bit unnatural and awkward, but with practice and sincerity it becomes a powerful experience.

2. Using Multiple Ethical Paradigms and Turbulence Theory Systematically

While many of the issues facing a new principal will be dealt with effectively by the five-step problem-solving dialogue, the mentor and protégé will almost certainly come face-to-face with much knottier problems. Ethical dilemmas cannot be addressed in a linear fashion because of their very nature. They are complex and linked to turbulence. This makes the use of multiple ethical paradigms and turbulence theory a central aspect of the leadership mentoring model. The mentor should reflect on the hypothetical case and the case study detailed earlier to see how this kind of dialogue can take place. In its most compact form there are four required steps:

1. Consider the turbulence level.
2. Consider the four ethical lenses.
3. Decide upon a course of action emphasizing one or more of the ethical lenses.
4. Estimate the change in turbulence that may result from the course of action.

Appropriate readings in the four ethical paradigms as well as turbulence theory and skills like the construction of turbulence gauges is central to the effective use of these combined theories.

Structure of the Leadership Mentoring Meetings

Without becoming too prescriptive, the Design Team believes that each meeting of the mentor and protégé should consist of these four elements in roughly this order:

1. Discussion and reflection on shared readings that are appropriate to the developmental needs of the protégé as described above. In the heat of busy days, it may seem like a luxury to devote time to the contemplation of readings. To believe this would be a serious mistake. The iterative cycle that adds the perspective of high-quality scholarly research to the minor and major crises of the school day is an imperative part of this program's design. The mentor is making a value statement by bringing the wider world of other practitioners and scholars to bear upon the issues facing the protégé. It is like saying, "Of course you are feeling like you are the only person facing these problems. But, while they are very real and do have a unique local flavor, you can turn to the experience of colleagues around the world to help you see new options. This is also a way of asking you to slow down, avoid panic, and allow a more systematic approach to work."

2. Problem solving of typical principal leadership issues. Here, the emphasis is on helping the new principal work through the technical issues that she or he will face, such as working with student schedules, budgeting, and planning for annual events. While this may not be as dramatic as dealing with the more nuanced issues of school leadership, the success of any principal's career is also dependent upon making these routine decisions. As the cycle of the first year goes by, it is anticipated that less and less time will need to be spent upon this kind of topic.

3. Problem solving of more difficult issues. This means employing the five-step dialogue to understand and respond to more serious issues facing principals. As the developmental stages of the principal show that mechanics will become easier to work through, highly effective leaders need to hone deeper skills. By raising issues at regular meetings and working them through with the five-step process, the mentor-protégé team can build skills and construct reasoned approaches to more challenging issues.

4. Problem solving of the most difficult type: Responding to authentic ethical dilemmas. This third category requires the use of multiple ethical paradigms and turbulence theory as detailed earlier. It may be that ethical dilemmas do not occur every week, but practice with the combined theories is essential if the protégé is to recognize them when they do arise and be able to confront them systematically. This means working on the process regularly as a team.

A Note on Meeting Format

The Design Team believes that both mentor and protégé will be busy professionals with many competing obligations. Perhaps the greatest risk to a program of leadership mentoring such as we envision is that it becomes a back-burner issue, losing out to more dramatic demands on the pair. If this happens, the program will only be a shell of what we intend and not worthy of the time and financial resources that the district has already devoted to it. That is why we have taken time to carefully map out the content that we feel is essential to the program and why we have structured the meetings carefully. We feel that an additional element is needed in planning each mentor-protégé meeting: the creation of a consistent agenda. The meeting agenda needs to contain each of the elements outlined above along with specific foci for each element. It should be prepared by the mentor, in conversation with the protégé with a completed copy for both parties before they meet. The school principal who does not hesitate to ask for detailed teacher lesson plans is well within his or her rights and should expect nothing less when it comes to his or her own learning program.

Going beyond Meetings: The Role of Outside Professional Affiliations in Leadership Mentoring

Most of this model naturally focuses on the relationship of the mentor-protégé pair. However, through this association, the protégé should be introduced to the wider world of educational leaders and connect to a network of new colleagues. One of the mentor's duties is to create such opportunities. Readings from quality professional journals are one way to open the door but that is only a start. Protégés need to be introduced to professional organizations that have a practitioner focus, such as the Association of Supervision and Curriculum Development (ASCD). Just as important, the protégé needs to connect to organizations that have a research agenda, such as the American Educational Research Association (AERA), and state and national educational organizations that have a scholarly and policy agenda, such as the Vermont Society for the Study of Education. Many districts support conference attendance for administrators. The Design Team believes that each year mentors and protégés should not only attend a conference but should also be encouraged to present as well and to include a mixture of practitioner and research conferences. In this way, the leadership mentoring program will diminish the risk that this experience will suffer from too much of a district-specific bent. Equally important, this approach will help veteran building leaders to build their own networks of learning and sharing because they too deserve such support and encouragement. If our district is to be an example of lifelong learning instead of a place where such high-sounding ideas are mere rhetoric, we must incorporate this element into our professional development program.

ATTAINMENT: ASSURING LEARNING THROUGH A WELL-ORGANIZED AND SYSTEMATICALLY REVIEWED PORTFOLIO

Of course, one of the attainment measures for the protégé is that person's success or failure to make a good home in this district. That is also the chief way that the program will be evaluated. We must remember that this program is designed to answer the problem of too much turnover of promising new principals. Yet, if we wait for this kind of ultimate evaluation, we will miss the opportunity to make the kinds of midcourse corrections at the individual and program levels that could be crucial. Therefore, the Design Team proposes a creative and systematic portfolio developed by each mentor-protégé team. The portfolio will be assembled and reviewed periodically by the team, and the collection of all portfolios will be reviewed by the leadership mentoring coordinator (see the "Structure" section of this report for further details on the role of the leadership mentoring coordinator).

Why a Portfolio Instead of Other Methods of Assessing Attainment?

A well-designed and well-maintained portfolio, unlike the results from a standardized test, is a living document. Portfolios reflect the rich variety of work that a person does over an extended period of time. In this way, they are more like a feature-length movie than a single snapshot that may not depict a person's work accurately. The fundamental thing to understand about a portfolio is that it must show *growth over time in all aspects of the protégé's professional life*. Below you will see the kinds of elements that need to be in the portfolio as well as the kinds of feedback and review envisioned for the portfolio system. When reading through this description, it may seem that this is a time-consuming process. That is an accurate observation. However, it is the very fact that the protégé and mentor need to spend time on the portfolio that adds to the quality of their reflections and increases the chance that their work will continue to grow and deepen. Just as both have made a commitment to professional development in the leadership mentoring program, both are committed to continually improving their performance through the vehicle of the portfolio.

Elements in Leadership Mentoring Portfolios

The portfolio is the central organizing device to demonstrate attainment in the leadership mentoring program. As such, it has three essential ingredients:

1. Document what is going on in the life of the protégé as it happens.
2. Reflections on key events and how they were handled.
3. Growth over time in facing typical and the more demanding events in the protégé's professional life.

- Written reflections on shared readings, especially how these readings relate to the protégé's immediate situation. These should be written each month and should be about two pages long.
- An evolving personal educational philosophy.[1] This should be written in succeeding drafts starting with the first semester of the mentoring process. A philosophy of education needs to be about five tightly written pages long.
- Written reflections on problem-solving issues.
- Artifacts including written documents, photos, videos, and computer-generated presentations showing achievement in the principalship with brief comments from the protégé and mentor.
- Audiotape of weekly experiences that includes comments and feedback from the mentor.
- Calendars with key school events and comment from the mentor and protégé.
- Agendas for all meetings.
- Periodic reflections on the protégé's development from the protégé's perspective and the perspective of the mentor. This should take place four times each school year. For both, the key issue is growth over time rather than judgmental evaluation.

Format

The portfolio may be three-dimensional or kept in virtual form on a computer hard drive or in other memory. Clearly, there are advantages to each. However, the privacy of the mentor-protégé relationship is paramount. Therefore, nothing that is personal in nature should be placed in the virtual portfolio.

STRUCTURE: THE ARCHITECTURE OF THE PROGRAM

While the Design Team realizes that a program as dynamic as leadership mentoring needs to evolve with experience, there is still a need to describe the responsibilities of key individuals and groups if the program is to have clear lines of authority and support. Below are the general responsibilities of superintendent, board, assistant superintendent for personnel and professional development, leadership mentoring coordinator, mentor, and protégé.

The Role of the Superintendent and School Board

- Review the work of all groups associated with leadership mentoring on a semiannual basis.
- Request program updates more regularly as events warrant.
- Request program amendments and adjustments as feedback indicates.

The Role of the Assistant Superintendent for Personnel and Professional Development

- Review the work of the leadership mentoring coordinator, mentors, and protégés in detail.
- Extend mentor-protégé pairs on annual basis as they are determined to be successful through review of portfolios.

- Assist leadership mentoring coordinator in helping mentor-protégé pairs who are having difficulty.
- Report program development to superintendent and school board annually.

The Role of the Leadership Mentoring Coordinator

- Organize the review of collected portfolios, analyze these, and provide feedback to each mentor-protégé pair as well as to the administration and school board.
- Engage mentors, match mentors to protégés.
- Secure external resources for the program, including application for external funding for such activities as participation in national conferences.
- Develop and conduct appropriate education of mentors.
- Engage in problem solving with mentors and protégés to assure effective experiences.
- Plan for mentor and protégé professional development during an annual one-week intensive workshop each summer.
- Collect feedback and build feedback into new program plans.

The Role of the Mentor

- Work under the guidance of the leadership mentor coordinator.
- Agree to a three-year commitment to the protégé.
- Maintain telephone contact with protégé of about three times each week for about 30 minutes per call.
- Meet with protégé two times per month for two hours each time. These meetings are to follow the outline of Leadership Mentoring Model above.
- Attend one national professional meeting aimed at practitioners.
- Attend one national professional meeting aimed at researchers.
- Engage in appropriate professional development during an annual one-week intensive workshop each summer.

The Role of the Protégé

- Work under the guidance of the leadership mentor coordinator.
- Agree to a three-year commitment to the mentoring relationship.
- Maintain telephone contact with mentor of about three times each week for about 30 minutes per call.
- Meet with mentor two times per month for two hours each time. These meetings are to follow the outline of Leadership Mentoring Model above.
- Attend one national professional meeting aimed at practitioners.
- Attend one national professional meeting aimed at researchers.
- Engage in appropriate professional development during an annual one-week intensive workshop each summer.

THE DESIGN TEAM REFLECTS UPON THE MODEL ONCE MORE

The model was ready for review by the board. It was important for the Design Team to explain why they were specific about some model elements and open-ended with others. Ronnie made the point. "Some people will wonder why we have not written a weekly lesson plan with topics for each mentor and protégé. We need to explain that we intend to provide guidance but not micromanagement."

"In this case our building codes metaphor will come in handy," Zbigniew pointed out. "What may also strike people strangely is our insistence on a specific problem-solving strategy and certainly our use of multiple ethical paradigms and turbulence theory as an organizing centerpiece. I mean, we've built up to this kind of thinking with the earlier reports, but now here it is in black and white." Warren, who had been rather reflective up until that moment, became animated. "We want choice, not default behaviors, because we believe in democracy, not brainwashing or blind obedience. Multiple ethical paradigms and turbulence theory is our best way to achieve that end because it forces the issue of ethical reasoning and the impact those choices have on levels of turbulence in the school." Warren's speech clearly connected with Francine. "Warren, that was beautiful. I can't believe that we didn't build that into our work yet. But maybe that is a kind of learning that this team is doing. We need to have a statement like yours at the end of this model to round off our plan." Warren, Ronnie, and Francine agreed to compose such a statement, which follows:

Conclusion: The Priorities of the Leadership Mentoring Model as an Example of Conscious Choice Rather Than Default Thinking

The Design Team believes that people ought to do what they do from choice, not by default. This is part of life in a free society. It is an axiom and sounds self-evident. Yet, when examined even in a cursory fashion, it is an idea with potentially revolutionary consequences. What does it mean to act out of choice, not default? It means not only being aware of the multiple options almost always available to us but also knowing ways to access those options so that they are functionally, pragmatically, and operationally possible. Seeing our choices and knowing how to move among the variety of open directions requires new opportunities, all of which are, or should be, norms to democratic living, but are too rarely more than abstraction. The Design Team believes that the practice of using multiple ethical paradigms makes options in ethical decision making real and that turbulence theory shows the possible consequences of alternative choices. It is our best strategy to help mentors and protégés consider how they can move from default behaviors to reflective, enlightened choices.

NOTE

1. Understanding one's own educational philosophy is a crucial step in becoming a grounded school leader and is more than an empty academic exercise. It involves clearly stating the kind of educational tradition that best defines you as a professional educator. This is a time for formal lan-

guage. The schools of educational philosophy commonly used in North America are finite. If this means more closely examining progressive education, essentialist education, perennialist education, and existentialist education, then that is part of the assignment for mentor and protégé. This is not a time to blindly sign on to one school of thought without considering the alternatives. Previous research into innovating schools (Gross 1998) has demonstrated that there is often a mixture of philosophies. The larger point is that one needs to assert one's position and not have events define one by default. This is not only crucial for the leader's own sense of security and identity, it is crucial for those with whom she or he works. A school or district leader who is clear on her or his own philosophical identity without descending into doctrinaire behaviors is a model for teachers, students, and families. While anyone's worldview may be attacked (and sooner or later all of our positions will be attacked), it is fairer for both our colleagues and ourselves to be clear in our beliefs.

Establishing our traditions is only a first step. Immersing oneself in the writings of that tradition is also required. At first, a busy new administrator may not think that there is time for such reading and thought. But the opposite is more likely the case: there is no time to waste in establishing some depth in one's traditions. This is because a deeper understanding of the writing of one's intellectual and philosophical forbears will arm the new administrator with powerful examples and ways of thinking through the difficult problems ahead. Instead of thinking of this as some esoteric assignment, think of this kind of reading as a coaching session with the world's best thinkers. Who wouldn't want that kind of help?

A case in point: At the end of my first semester of teaching high school social studies, I was asked to meet with our school's director. It seemed that students in my classes received grades that were somewhat higher than the ones they received in the classrooms of some of my colleagues. I understood that a question may arise regarding my sense of rigor. In my opinion, my classes were very demanding, but they were also student centered and oriented toward giving all students credit for being able to learn effectively if only I approached them as intelligent human beings. Even with a sure sense that I had acted appropriately, I worried as the day for my meeting drew nearer. I called my own mentor, Professor Norman Kaner. He was a dear friend and someone who had encouraged me during my undergraduate days as a history major at Temple University. Norman's reaction underscores my point. "Steve, you must get hold of the books that have influenced you. You have great reasons for teaching in your way and for assigning those grades. But your school's director is not a mind reader, and it is up to you to show how you think about teaching, where your ideals come from, and why this is not a case of low standards. Your standards are really very high, but you must make that clear with evidence. Get out your evidence."

With that, I started to reread works by the writers who influenced me, like John Holt, Paolo Freire, and Herbert Kohl. This exercise proved the obvious to me: of course I was not alone. Clearly, many reasonable and conscientious teachers had lived their professional lives guided by the same stars. My intuitive way of being in the classroom placed me within a family of thinkers. When the meeting finally came, a strange thing happened. Far from spouting off some artificial polemic filled with bombastic quotes from my favorite authors, I went in the opposite direction. I was very calm and even happy for the chance for meaningful dialogue. I wanted to understand what concerns existed about my teaching and grading. When my turn came to explain myself, I felt relaxed and enthusiastic all at once. What I wanted was a classroom where people worked very hard and pushed further than they thought possible and were rewarded by authentic discoveries rather than grades. I taught that if students threw themselves into their studies, powerful learning would result, and good grades would follow. I doubt that I won over many others in the faculty or administration. However, I did carve out a space for myself that was respected. I am reasonably certain that no such space would have existed without the help of those whose shoulders I had the honor to stand upon.

Whatever their philosophical tradition(s), the mentor and protégé must push further to define that position in light of democracy and ethical reasoning.

CHAPTER 6

Implementation of the Leadership Mentoring Program

So much had happened since the first discussions between Betty and Antonio months before. The Design Team took their charges to heart, worked in a highly professional manner, presented well, and took criticism well. The result was a program that responded to authentic district needs, reflected research, and based its approach on promising theoretical concepts. On top of that, the program model was clear and understandable to the public and seemed possible to put into practice. All of this meant that the problem Betty and Antonio shared about nurturing and keeping the best possible building leaders seemed like one they could respond to as soon as the new budget was passed. However, before any new program could be brought to life, the Design Team needed to go to work on one last but essential facet: program implementation. In their final monthly meeting, the group took time to contemplate their approach to this challenge.

"I would like most to hear from the district people on this one." Zbigniew was sure that local habit would be important when it came time to put a plan into action. His experience in other organizations taught him that ignoring local institutional cultures could spell the end of any plan, even one that had as much promise as their leadership mentoring program.

The district representatives smiled at each other and at Zbigniew. They were thinking along the same lines and were prepared to share their perspectives. "First, if I am inferring correctly, you are trying to avoid the mistakes that other groups made in getting their work into our schools," Ronnie was on the right track and knew it. "That's a good start. It's not as though our school culture will kill new ideas, just the opposite. However, there needs to be some recognition of all of the groups. In this case, our mentoring program is not so different from the one we have for teachers, except for the professional meetings our plan envisions. In this case, it might be wise for us to ask that the district apply for funds so that a group of teachers might attend meetings so that we can have a greater benefit of knowledge for more people. But that is a detail. What I have been thinking about is a larger issue. This program of mentoring leaders cannot exist in isolation or it will be an appendage. I am asking—and anyone who has worked on our school's curriculum, instruction, and assessment programs will ask—how is this program going to be integrated into the rest of our work?"

Ashley had the same idea. "Ronnie, that's the way I am seeing it too. What I did was to look for a resource that might help us to see just how ready we are to get this program started. I found a checklist for leadership mentoring (table 6.1) (Gross 2004) and suggest that we look through it together since it addresses your issues and others that are important for us, Betty, and the board to consider."

This led the Design Team to examine the eight issues in the checklist and make relevant comments after each item:

1. *Support from the top.* This was easily answered. The program started from the two people in highest leadership positions in the district, the superintendent of schools and the school board chair. Support from the top was clearly in place.
2. *Room in the budget.* This was not accomplished but seemed to be reasonable. The leadership mentoring coordinator would be a new position but it could be a part-time one since there were not normally enough new principals to warrant a full-time position. Beyond that, the Design Team expected that costs could be offset in part by savings in recruiting new building leaders.
3. *A formal role for the mentor.* The work of the Design Team assured a formal role for the mentor and a structured set of expectations and supports for these professionals.

Table 6.1. Leadership Mentoring Readiness Table

Checklist Item	Item in Place	Item Easily Put in Place	This Item Will Take Time
1. Support from the top			
2. Room in the budget			
3. A formal role for the mentor			
4. A formalized process			
5. A strong commitment to the reform process of the school			
6. A strong commitment to the professional development of the new principal			
7. Commitment to adequate amounts of time			
8. Use of the mentor-protégé relationship during an appropriate phase of the school's reform cycle			

Source: Reprinted with permission from Gross (2004).

4. *A formalized process.* The Design Team was likewise sure that its model would support the protégés and mentors without locking them into a micromanaged program. There was also room for feedback and corrections to the mentoring process.
5. *A strong commitment to the reform process of the school.* This was an area of concern for everyone on the Design Team. It was not really a problem of having the mentoring program at odds with the district's work in school reform; it was more a

matter that the Design Team had not yet contemplated. This required further work.
6. *A strong commitment to the professional development of the new principal.* The development of the protégé was the top priority of the Design Team and was supported by all of the school board members and district administrators. Again, this was an easy item to check off.
7. *Commitment to adequate amounts of time.* While no one could guarantee that three years was enough time for a mentor and protégé to work together, this was at the top end of the research that the Design Team used to fashion its work. The weekly telephone calls, bimonthly meetings, attendance at annual conferences, and summer workshops were likewise more frequent than in much of the research. However, the group was more than willing to err on the side of generous amounts of time given the significance of the program. They could gradually adjust each of the time elements as feedback and experience taught them that less time would do.
8. *Use of the mentor-protégé relationship during an appropriate phase of the school's reform cycle.* Just as number 5 above was an area of concern, this item also made the Design Team pause to consider.

Ashley brought the group back into focus after the members agreed upon the district's condition in each of the eight items. "This was a kind of eye-opener for me. It is just so easy for us to work in a vacuum and not know it. We started our work by admitting that even the best mentoring program is only a part of leadership induction. Now we have to go further; even the best leadership induction is only part of a much wider program of deep and sustained innovation leading to ongoing reform of our educational program. Based upon this perspective, we need to say something that would help the district implement the leadership mentoring program in such a way that it knits together mentoring and our reform program."

The implementation plan drafted by the Design Team reflected just this tack.

IMPLEMENTING THE LEADERSHIP MENTORING PROGRAM IN OUR DISTRICT

First, the Design Team believes that the district needs to think through its own readiness to start a leadership mentoring program. After reviewing a readiness checklist (Gross 2004), we found that most but not all of the key elements of support are in place. For instance, there is excellent support for the program from district and board leaders, a carefully designed plan with formal roles for both mentors and protégés. Having said this, the Design Team must point out that there is not yet a clear connection between the district's reform process and the mentoring program. This means that the mentoring program does not yet have enough to do with all of the efforts that we are making to improve our schools, especially in the areas of curriculum, instruction, and assessment. To correct this gap, we propose the following steps:

1. We need to come together as an educational community and consider our shared educational philosophy. What of the progressive education movement do we hold dear? Where is essentialism or perennialism important to us? Is there room in our schools for an existentialist point of view? These may sound like esoteric questions, but the Design Team is certain that the shared philosophy is highly practical. When we know what our shared ideals are, we can then make sure that we are consistent. We do not expect to be purely one school of philosophy or another (Gross 1998). In fact, it may be desirable for the district to have different academies inside our present schools so that more perspectives can be represented. Our point is that clarity of perspective must come first.

2. Once we have a sense of where we stand, we should see to it that our curriculum, instruction, and assessment are aligned with our philosophy. Just as we would not recommend a principal candidate to run a school whose philosophy was diametrically opposed to her own, we should not hire someone who is ill prepared to assure a smooth flow of philosophy throughout the school's learning agenda. This means seeing that shared philosophy in curriculum, instruction, and assessment to the greatest extent possible.

   This may sound abstract but we ask the board to consider the pressures we are feeling now from the state and federal governments in the form of increased high-stakes testing. What chance do our schools have to maintain local innovation if leaders at the building level cannot see how these new tests may conflict with the priorities we have established? We can easily see how dialogues about this subject could arise during mentor-protégé meetings, so we believe that this is a vital step to take in program implementation.
3. We need open forums to continue the discussion of our shared educational philosophy so that we can change and adjust as new people come into our district.
4. We must continue to review the specifics of the leadership mentoring model to make sure that the kinds of people whom we ask to become mentors and the content of the program itself reflect our reform program.

Once the district attends to the four items just detailed, a formal motion is needed to adopt the model. Specifically, these steps need to be taken in full session:

1. A budget must be proposed for the first year of operation.
2. A program coordinator must be hired, remembering that this is likely going to be a part-time position.

3. The board and superintendent must empower the program coordinator to identify the first group of mentors. In finding new mentors care needs to be taken to assure the mentors have a philosophy compatible with that of the district. We may have such individuals among our current leaders, but if not, other options are available to us. For instance, we might contact recent retirees and local or regional higher-education adjunct faculty, or coordinate our work with neighboring districts.
4. The Design Team also suggests that area institutions of higher education be contacted to explore the creation of a pilot program in mentoring. By partnering with institutions such as this, two goals could be realized. First, the Randolph District could have help in designing and delivering mentor education and program evaluation through the cooperation of committed higher-education faculty. The second advantage to such a plan would be the possibility for mentors to earn formal recognition for their increased expertise in the form of a certification of advanced study (CAS). Such an award would help participating administrators to earn recertification credit and offer a tangible reward for their participation in mentoring service.
5. The Design Team believes that if the Randolph School District decides to move in the direction of differentiated staffing for administrators, service in the leadership mentoring program should count as significant evidence of senior administrative achievement. Indeed, the mentoring role, because it is generative in nature, could become an integral element of a senior administrator's duties.
6. In order to assure consistent high-quality communication about the program, the Design Team suggests the creation of a special leadership mentoring website that is open to everyone. This site can contain important program developments, invitations to public meetings, and presentations. This site should

also include relevant links to other sites where leadership mentoring is discussed.

By taking these steps, the district will be ready to begin the mentoring process as soon as a new principal is hired. It does represent a good deal of advance work but it is our best shot at making sure that we do not bring new people along without guidance and support.

Conclusion: The Design Team's Closing Meeting

It was not a typical meeting for the Design Team, at least not in the sense that a next report was due. That was behind them after the implementation plan was submitted to the Randolph board. This meeting was more of an acknowledgment of a basic group dynamic process requirement, the need for closure. Not everyone would have used that word, but everyone understood the point. Months of close, often intense, work was over. Tight time lines and demanding results were checked off their to-do list. Much was learned by each member. Just as important, the group learned to trust one another and to respect the wondrous skills that surfaced as if by magic, just because of their growing faith in themselves and in each other.

Betty looked around the table and began the meeting. "You know, the textbooks on group process refer to this as the termination phase. Don't worry, no one is getting fired!" There was a moment of nervous laughter. "That is an awkward word for what you may be feeling just now since we are at a kind of departure point for the Design Team. It may have been only four months since we brought you together..."

"It seems like four years to me!" Ronnie couldn't help interrupting with a joke. Everyone laughed and thought of their own difficult moments during the project's development.

"All right, I know what you mean. Seriously, though, there was a phase of meeting each other, establishing agreements on how to do the work, debating, and producing good results. In my view, you've got a highly functioning team. Now, you're finished and it's time to move on. I want to tell you how much your plans will help us turn around the problem of losing promising new administrators."

"That's not all." Antonio was itching to share a surprise. "The board, Betty, and Ronnie have been discussing the next step. After approving the budget for leadership mentoring, we needed to find a coordinator. Ronnie, why don't you tell them?"

"Right. Well, it seems as though it's time to move into action, and it's also time for me to blend mentoring in with my other responsibilities. Minus some that can be delegated, right, Betty?" The superintendent nodded pleasantly. "I loved the planning stages but now I want to dive into the building stage. We spoke about making a program with building codes, not micromanaged, cookie-cutter-house designs. I'll need to work through the details to turn our district's specific conditions and the Design Team's plan into a congenial blend."

That announcement broke the ice and led to continued involvement for other members of the Design Team over time. Sam became pivotal in the effort to link the leadership mentoring program to Acropolis University, just as the implementation plan envisioned. Zbigniew offered to help in fundraising with foundations and area business leaders. Ashley's role as assistant superintendent was written into the plan. Warren became the first mentor later that spring when an opening in an elementary school led to hiring a first-time principal. Francine, not to be left behind, volunteered to help with the new website and to cohost open-house meetings on mentoring with Zbigniew. They all had become more committed to the concept of mentoring than they realized.

Turning out the lights after the meeting and walking out of the door with Betty, Antonio turned to her with a question. "So, are you still wondering about your decision to stay in here in Randolph?"

"Antonio, four months ago, all I saw was danger. Now, I see real opportunity. Amazing!"

"Amazing? Trust, hard work, innovation, dialogue. Well, maybe it is just a bit amazing."

This book, like other long projects that I have undertaken, has been a unique journey from the early planning to this moment when I need to close. I realized nearly at once that our times required a new perspective in solving the problem of nurturing new leaders into the job of school principal, and I am grateful to those who have contributed so much to this field and whose work has taken us to the place where such a departure can be suggested.

First, I believe that the problem is not simply one of describing the program that needs to be established by the professionals in a school district. The Design Team and all that they discovered as they responded to each of their charges are essential ingredients to the work of building a leadership mentoring program. Their work demonstrates the need to integrate multiple perspectives, work interdependently, and continually remember that the public's perspective is essential in public education.

Next, the literature is used by the Design Team to understand the current state of thinking about this topic. Their review of the literature is parallel to that of doctoral students learning about the state of the scholarly discussions in their proposed dissertation field. This means understanding that our view of the need for mentoring and how to respond to that need evolves with time and that the Randolph District's approach amounts to a contribution to the field of scholarship as much as it responds to local conditions. In this way, I have tried to show one way that local-practitioner efforts can connect with relevant scholarship. This is too infrequently accomplished, much to the detriment of both practitioners and researchers.

In their next step, the Design Team members reached a watershed moment when they realized that their program needed a theoretical framework. Through their example, I have tried to make the case for centering leadership mentoring on the conceptual strength of multiple ethical paradigms and turbulence theory because I believe that the ability to resolve deep ethical dilemmas is central to the school leader's job. As the Design Team discovered, the mechanics of the job must be understood and mastered, but that is not enough to qualify someone as a leader.

Yet, they did not stop with this step because they understood that everyone in the system needed to see how such leadership mentoring, sustained over several years and centered with such a framework, looked in practice. The case study is useful in two ways, therefore. It demonstrates that such a program is possible and can be highly effective in the real world of school leadership. It also shows that multiple ethical paradigms and turbulence theory are used in such a successful leadership mentoring practice.

The Design Team simply took the next step by fashioning a model program where mentors and protégés studied this approach systematically. The model further helps districts integrate content, interactive learning, and attainment in a mutually reinforcing way. The content includes the same learning that the Design Team experienced as they became seasoned in the concepts and research in the field. This brings mentors and protégés into the developing landscape of leadership mentoring as full participants and raises mentoring to the level of education rather than mere training. Instead of didactic instruction, this model has opted for interactive learning that includes the deepening of the mentor's own understanding of leadership. That is why so much of the work of the mentor and protégé is embedded in a systematically organized dialogue. No one in this system has arrived at a final destination of full awareness. Everyone is in the throes of growth and development. Perhaps by recognizing that the leaders of the system are learners, more empathy and understanding of all learners will result. Congruent with this kind of content and interactive learning is the protégé's portfolio, which needs to show continuing growth over time.

I am convinced that the model passes the test of reasonableness in two crucial ways. First, it is reasonable because it is responsive to the needs of the district. The model represents a robust program of development for new principals that can be sustained through continued feedback and new information. Second, it is reasonable because we have evidence from the field that such deep commitments can occur. It is not too much to ask. The better question may be, if any one district supports new principals in such a thorough manner with such good results, why can't every new principal enjoy the same level of support and increased chances for success?

Finally, the work of the Design Team moved to program implementation. Here again their work diverges from the typical practice of recommending a linear approach to program adoption. Their use of a leadership mentoring readiness checklist reveals that the district has many pieces in place, such as support for the program from the superintendent and school board. However, there is a major hole in the strategic thinking of the district since there is no clear connection between the mentoring project and the rest of the district's reform efforts. Thus, the Design Team attempted to push the district to build a bridge between the two and thereby strengthen both the emergent leadership mentoring program and the larger reform agenda. Without such a move, there is every chance that school leaders will work with a serious blind spot. The chances for holistic thinking such as this seem improved with a team approach to program development phased in over several months.

To achieve an understanding and security in school leadership, I have supported long-lasting contact between the mentor and protégé. If we believe that wise leaders move their schools in times of open opportunity and stand firmly against the excesses of intrusion when cherished local innovations are threatened, then we have depicted a depth of understanding, courage, and moral reasoning that cannot come easily or swiftly. This kind of leader emerges most probably with time and the help of a guide who is also anxious to see the world of education in new ways. It would be a mistake, however, to imagine that this standard cannot be achieved because it demands too much of systems and their professionals. The case study showed just the opposite. In addition, scores of our graduate students at Temple University, most of whom are busy practicing administrators, have learned how to use multiple ethical paradigms and turbulence theory through the pioneering teaching of my colleague, Joan P. Shapiro, and have demonstrated their growing expertise at national and international conferences.

I am arguing for a mentoring program with direction and clarity. I do not believe in a generic approach to the work because I do not believe that externally imposed standards can turn someone into a competent educational leader. Rather, one needs to become a responsible educator. That implies dedication to the craft, art, and ethics of our profession motivated by an inner drive to serve. My highest aspiration for this book is that it might help us bring into office and nurture the next generation of such a leadership corps. That is a requirement, in my opinion, if we are to see truly new, democratic-ethical educational leadership blossom in this turbulent era.

References

Aiken, J. (2002). The socialization of new principals: Another perspective on principal retention. *Education Leadership Review, 3*(1), 32–40.

Apple, M. W. (1988). *Teachers and texts: A political economy of class and gender relations in education.* New York: Routledge & Kegan Paul.

Archer, J. (2002). Novice principals put huge strain on NYC schools. *Education Week, 38,* 1, 15.

Bakhtin, M. (1981). *The dialogic imagination.* Austin: University of Texas Press.

Bank Street College (1992). *The Principals' Institute 1990–1992,* New York City Board of Education.

Barnett, B. G. (1991). School-university collaboration: A fad or the future of administration preparation? *Planning and Changing, 21,* 146–157.

Barnett, B. G. (1995). Developing reflection and expertise: Can mentors make the difference? *Journal of Educational Administration, 33,* 45–59.

Beauchamp, T. L., & Childress, J. F. (1984). Morality, ethics, and ethical theories. In P. Sola (Ed.), *Ethics, education, and administrative decisions: A book of readings* (pp. 39–67). New York: Peter Lang.

Beck, L. G. (1994). *Reclaiming educational administration as a caring profession.* New York: Teachers College Press.

Begley, P. T. (Ed.). (1999). *Values and educational leadership.* Albany: State University of New York Press.

Belenky, M., Clinchy, B., Goldberger, N., & Tarule, J. (1986). *Women's ways of knowing.* New York: Basic Books.

Blackman, M., & Fenwick, L. (2000). The principalship. *Education Week on the Web.* http://www.edweek.org.

Bolman, L., Deal, T. (1993). *The path to school leadership: A portable mentor.* Newbury Park: Corwin Press.

Boon, S. L. Z. (1998). Principalship mentoring in Singapore: Who and what benefits? *Journal of School Administration, 36,* 29–43.

Bowles, S., & Gintis, H. (1988). *Democracy and capitalism.* New York: Basic Books.

Brown, K., Anfara, V., Hartman, K., Mahar, R., & Mills, R. (2001). *Professional development of middle-level principals.* Paper presented at the Annual Meeting of the American Educational Research Association, Seattle, Washington.

Bundy, B., & McKay, B. (2004). Beginning principals' mentoring program, Prince George's County, Maryland. London: UK: National College for School Leadership.

Calabrese, R. L., & Tucker-Ladd, P. R. (1991). The principal and assistant principal: A mentoring relationship. *NASSP Bulletin, 75,* 67–74.

Capasso, R. L., & Daresh, J. C. (2001). *The school administration handbook: Leading, mentoring, and participating in the internship program.* Thousand Oaks, CA: Corwin Press.

Cohn, K. C., & Sweeny, R. C. (1992). Principal mentoring programs: Are school districts providing the leadership? Paper presented at the Annual Meeting of the American Educational Research Association, San Francisco, CA (ERIC Document Reproduction Service ED 345376).

Coleman, M., et al. (1996). Re-thinking training for principals: The role of mentoring. Paper presented at the Annual Meeting of the American Educational Research Association, New York. (ERIC Document Reproduction Service ED 397479)

Cordeiro, P., & Smith-Sloan, L. (1995). Apprenticeships for administrative interns: Learning to talk like a principal. Paper presented at the Annual Meeting of the American Educational Research Association, San Francisco, CA.

Crocker, C., & Harris, S. (2002). Facilitating growth of administrative practitioners as mentors. *Journal of Research for Educational Leader, 1,* 5–20.

Crow, G. M. and Matthews, L. J. (1998). *Finding one's way: How mentoring can lead to dynamic partnership.* Thousand Oaks, CA: Corwin.

Curtis, D. (2004). The freshman principal. Edutopia Online, printed from the Internet site: http://glef.org/ php/article.php?id=Art_1000.

Daloz, L. A. (1983). Mentors: Teachers who make a difference. *Change, 5,* 24–27.

Daresh, J. C. (2001). *Leaders helping leaders: A practical guide to administrative mentoring* (2nd ed.). Thousand Oaks, CA: Corwin.

Daresh, J. C., Playko, M. A. (1992) *The professional development of school administrators: Pre-service, induction and in-service application.* Boston: Allyn & Bacon.

Daresh, J., & Playko, M. (1993). *Benefits of a mentoring program for aspiring administrators.* Paper presented at the Annual Meeting of the American Association of School Administrators, Orlando, FL. (ERIC Document Reproduction Service ED354603)

Delgado, R. (1995). *Critical race theory: The cutting edge.* Philadelphia: Temple University Press.

Dewey, J. (1934). *A Common Faith.* New Haven: Yale University Press.

Dukess, L. (2001). *Meeting the leadership challenge: Designing effective principal mentoring programs.* New York: New Visions for Public Schools.

Dunavin, R. (2004). School leaders are not developed equally: Principals' and assistant principals' differing induction and professional development experiences. Paper presented at the 2004 Annual Meeting of the American Educational Research Association, San Diego, CA.

Enz, B. J. (1992). Guidelines for selecting mentors and creating an environment for mentoring. In T. Bey and C. Holmes (Eds.), *Mentoring contemporary principles and issues* (pp. 65–77). Reston, VA: Association of Teacher Educators.

Erasmus, M., and Westhuizen, P. C. van der (1994). Guidelines for the professional development of school principals by means of a mentoring system in a developing country. Paper presented at the International Intervisitation Programme, Buffalo, NY. (ERIC Document Reproduction Service ED371440)

Foucault, M. (1983). On the genealogy of ethics: An overview of work in progress. In H. L. Dreyfus and P. Rabinow (Eds.), *Michel Foucault: Beyond structuralism and hermeneutics*, 2nd ed. (pp. 229–52). Chicago: University of Chicago Press.

Freire, P. (1970). *Pedagogy of the oppressed.* (M. B. Ramos, Trans.) New York: Continuum.

Gehrke, N. J., & Kay, R. S. (1984). The socialization of beginning teachers through mentor-protégé relationships. *Journal of Teacher Education, 35*, 21–24.

Geismar, T. J., Morris, J. D., & Lieberman, M. G. (2000). Selecting mentors for principalship interns. *Journal of School Leadership, 10,* 233–247.

REFERENCES

Gilligan, C. (1982). *In a different voice: Psychological theory and women's development.* Cambridge, MA: Harvard University Press.

Gilligan, C., Ward, J. V., & Taylor, J. M. (1988). *Mapping the moral domain.* Cambridge, MA: Harvard University Press.

Giroux, H. A. (1994). Educational leadership and school administrators: Rethinking the meaning of democratic public culture. In T. Mulkeen, N. H. Cambron-McCabe, & B. Anderson (Eds.) *Democratic leadership: The changing context of administrative preparation* (pp. 31–47). Norwood, NJ: Ablex.

Glaser, B., & Straus, A. L. (1967). *The discovery of grounded theory: Strategies for qualitative research.* Chicago: Aldine.

Goodlad, J. I., Soder, R., & Sirotnik, K. A. (Eds.). (1990). *The moral dimension of teaching.* San Francisco: Jossey-Bass.

Goodwin, D. K. (1994). *No ordinary time. Franklin and Eleanor Roosevelt: The home front in World War II.* New York: Simon & Schuster.

Greene, M. (1988). *The dialectic of freedom.* New York: Teachers College Press.

Gross, S. J. (1998). *Staying centered: Curriculum leadership in a turbulent era.* Alexandria, VA: Association for Supervision and Curriculum Leadership.

Gross, S. J. (1999). Life After Moses: The fate of selected innovative institutions beyond the transformational leader. Paper presented at the Annual Meeting of the American Educational Research Association, Montreal.

Gross, S. J. (2000, October). *From turbulence to tidal wave: Understanding the unraveling of reform at one innovative and diverse urban elementary school for children at risk.* Paper presented at the Northeast Educational Research Association annual conference, New York.

Gross, S. J. (2002). Passing a torch: Sustaining change through leadership mentoring at one reforming high school. *Journal of In-Service Education, 28,* 35–56.

Gross, S. J. (2004). *Promises kept: Sustaining school and district leadership in a turbulent era.* Alexandria, VA: Association for Supervision and Curriculum Leadership.

Gross, S. J., & Shapiro, J. P. (2004). Using multiple ethical paradigms and turbulence theory in response to administrative dilemmas. *International Studies in Educational Administration, 32,* 47–62.

Gross, S. J., & Shapiro, J. P. (2005). Our new era requires a new deel: Towards democratic ethical educational leadership. *UCEA Review, XLVII*(3), 1–4.

Gryskiewicz, S. S. (1999). *Positive turbulence*. San Francisco: Jossey-Bass.

Haberman, M., & Dill, V. (1999, January). Selecting star principals for schools serving children in poverty. *Instructional Leader, 12*(1), 11–12.

Hart, A. W. (1991). Leader succession and socialization: A synthesis. *Review of Educational Research, 61,* 451–474.

Hart, A., & Bredeson, P. (1996). *The principalship: A theory of professional learning and practice*. New York: McGraw-Hill.

Hay, J. (1995). *Transformational mentoring: Creating developmental alliances for changing organizational cultures*. London: McGraw-Hill.

Head, T., Reiman, A., Thies, & Sprinthall, L. (1992). The reality of mentoring: Complexity in process and function. In T. Bey and C. Holmes (Eds.), *Mentoring contemporary principles and issues* (pp. 5–24). Reston, VA: Association of Teacher Educators.

Hopkins, G. (1998). Help wanted: Qualified principal. *Education World*. Retrieved, November 10, 2004. http://www.educationworld.com/a_admin/admin067.shtml.

Interstate School Leaders Licensure Consortium (ISLLC). (1996). *Standards for school leaders*. Washington, DC: Council of Chief State School Officers.

Kay, R. S. (1992). Mentor management: Emphasizing the human in managing human resources. In T. Bey and C. Holmes (Eds.), *Mentoring contemporary principles and issues* (pp. 51–63). Reston, VA: Association of Teacher Educators.

Kohlberg, L. (1981). *The philosophy of moral development: Moral stages and the idea of justice*. (Vol. 1). San Francisco, CA: Harper & Row.

Lashway, L. (2003). Inducting school leaders. Eugene, OR: CEPM Clearinghouse on Educational Management (ERIC Digest 170). http://eric.uoregon.edu/publications/digests/digest170.html

Levinson, D. J., Darrow, C. N., Klein, E. B., Levinson, M. H., & McKee, B. (1978). *The seasons of a man's life*. New York: Ballantine.

Lincoln, Y. S. (1999). *Mentoring in the moment*. Paper presented at the Southwest Educational Research Association, San Antonio, TX.

Malone, R. J. (2001). Principal mentoring. CEPM Clearinghouse on Educational Management (ERIC Digest 149). http://eric.uoregon.edu/publications/digests/digest 149.html

Maslow, A. (1970). *Motivation and personality* (2nd ed.). New York: Harper & Row.

Matters, P. (1994). Mentoring partnerships: Key to leadership success for principals and managers. Paper prepared for the Annual Meeting of the International Congress for School Effectiveness and Improvement, Melbourne, Victoria, Australia. (ERIC Document Reproduction Service ED366113)

Mertz, N. T. (2004). What's a mentor, anyway? *Educational Administration Quarterly, 40,* 541–560.

Morgan, G. (1997). *Images of organization.* Thousand Oaks, CA.: Sage.

Muse, I. D., Wasden, F. D., & Thomas, G. J. (1988). *The mentor principal: Handbook.* Provo, UT: Brigham Young University Press.

National Association of Elementary School Principals (NAESP), National Association of Secondary School Principals (NASSP), Educational Research Service (ERS). (1998). *Is there a shortage of qualified candidates for openings in the principalship?*

Nelson, B. (2003). Help for first-time principals. *Education Gazette.* Retrieved from www.edgazette.govt.nz/articles/show_articles.cgi?

Noddings, N. (1984/1992). *Caring: A feminine approach to ethics and moral education.* Berkeley, CA: University of California Press.

Paskey, R. J. (1989). The principal as mentor, partner of assistant principals, *NASSP Bulletin, 73,* 95–98.

Pavan, B. (1986). Mentors and mentoring functions perceived as helpful to certified aspiring and incumbent female and male public school administrators. Paper presented at the Annual Meeting of the American Educational Research Association, San Francisco, CA. (ERIC Document Reproduction Service ED 269884)

Peel, H., et al. (1998). Improving leadership preparation programs through a school, university, and professional organization partnership, *NASSP Bulletin, 82,* 26–34.

Playko, M. A. (1991). Mentors for administrators: Support for the instructional leader. *Theory into Practice, 30,* 124–127.

Purpel, D. E., & Shapiro, S. (1995). *Beyond liberation and excellence: Reconstructing the public discourse on education.* Westport, CT: Bergin & Garvey.

Restine, L. N. (1993). Mentoring: Assisting and developing the new generation of leaders. *People and Education, 1,* 42–51.

Schein, E. H. (1978). *Career dynamics: Matching individual and organizational needs.* Reading, MA: Addison-Wesley.

Sergiovanni, T. J. (1992). *Moral leadership: Getting to the heart of school improvement.* San Francisco: Jossey-Bass.

Shapiro, J. P., & Smith-Rosenberg, C. (1989). The "other voices" in contemporary ethical dilemmas: The value of the new scholarship on women in the teaching of ethics. *Women's Studies International Forum, 12(2),* 199–211.

Shapiro, J. P. & Stefkovich, J. A. (2001, 2005). *Ethical leadership and decision making in education: Applying theoretical perspectives to complex dilemmas.* 2nd ed. Mahwah, NJ: Lawrence Erlbaum Associates.

Southworth, G., (1995). Reflections on mentoring for new school leaders. *Journal of Educational Administration, 33,* 17–28.

Starratt, R. J. (1994). *Building an ethical school.* London: Falmer Press.

Straus, A. L., Corbin, J. (1998). Grounded theory methodology. In N. K. Denzin, & Y. S. Lincoln (Eds.) *Strategies of qualitative inquiry.* Thousand Oaks, CA: Sage.

Strike, K. A. (1991). The moral role of schooling in liberal democratic society. In G. Grant (Ed.), *Review of research in education* (pp. 413–483). Washington, DC: American Educational Research Association.

Strike, K. A., Haller, E. J., & Soltis, J. F. (1998). *The ethics of school administration.* 2nd ed. New York: Teachers College Press.

United States Department of Labor (2005). *Occupational outlook handbook, 2004–2005 edition.* Bulletin 2750. Washington, DC: U.S. Government Printing Office.

Walker, A., & Stott, K. (1994). Mentoring programs for aspiring principals: Getting a solid start. *NASSP Bulletin, 78,* 72–77.

Wilmore, E. L. (1995). It's not easy being green: Mentoring for the first year principal. *NASSP Bulletin, 79,* 91–96.

Wunsch, M. (1994). *Mentoring: Making an impact on individuals and institutions.* San Francisco: Jossey-Bass.

Zachary, L. J. (2000). *The mentor's guide.* San Francisco: Jossey-Bass.

About the Author

Steven Jay Gross is associate professor of educational leadership and policy studies at Temple University, Philadelphia, Pennsylvania. Gross's teaching, books, articles, and research activities focus on initiating and sustaining deep, democratic reform in schools and turbulence theory. His books include *Staying Centered: Curriculum Leadership in a Turbulent Era* (1998) and *Promises Kept: Sustaining School and District Leadership in a Turbulent Era* (2004). Gross served as editor of ASCD's Curriculum Handbook series and is a senior fellow at the Vermont Society for the Study of Education. Along with colleagues across North America and Australia, Gross is a leading figure in a movement called the New DEEL (Democratic-Ethical Educational Leadership), which seeks to lift education beyond the top-down accountability movement toward the values of democracy, social justice, and authentic learning.